BEAT THE COPS

THE GUIDE
TO
FIGHTING
YOUR TRAFFIC TICKET
AND WINNING

ALEX CARROLL

BEAT THE COPS

THE GUIDE
TO
FIGHTING
YOUR TRAFFIC TICKET
AND WINNING

BY ALEX CARROLL

PUBLISHED BY ACECO PUBLISHERS

Library of Congress Number:
Carroll, Alex L.
Beat The Cops: The Guide To Fighting Your Traffic Ticket And Winning by Alex Carroll
94–71428

WHAT'S IN THIS BOOK
(Table Of Contents)

ABOUT THE AUTHOR

Who is Alex Carroll and why did he write this book?

It all started some years ago when the author first received that cherished symbol of young adulthood, a driver's license. Like most of us he learned the hard way that being able to spot a cop, before the cop spotted him, was a very vital driving skill. He learned that cops like to hide behind bushes with radar guns in hand, and that they get a big kick out of stalking unsuspecting speeders from patrol planes. He was especially tickled to learn about those photo radar machines that take your picture, which is mailed to you along with a ticket, if you were allegedly exceeding the speed limit. He doesn't know about *your* driver training class, but his sure didn't teach or warn him about these road hazards.

While learning, he accumulated 16 tickets, for an impressive array of violations. Now, you might suggest that he was a careless driver. How else would he have received that many citations? It's true. He was careless. But only in the sense that he did not watch for cops. In many cases the officer's charges were exaggerated, or even completely false. Even when their charges were totally accurate, he hadn't done anything to endanger or harm anyone or anything in any way. So he thought to himself, "This is not fair. I don't deserve this. I can't afford this. Can I fight this? If so, how?"

So began his battle against "the traffic citation." His efforts have been very successful. At last count he has overturned or nullified 10 tickets and in the process found that winning was actually easy. The first time the author walked into a courtroom to fight a ticket, he was scared to death, not to mention completely lost. It became apparent to him that his fellow ticket recipients were as scared and lost as he was.

After challenging and successfully overturning a few tickets, he found himself helping others with their citations. It was at that point he realized that he was saving people a lot of money and, more importantly, putting smiles on their faces. Now that may sound corny, but it is a great feeling when someone walks up to you on the street and says: "Thank you very much for your help. You saved my day." That's why he wrote this book: The desire to help as many people as he can in challenging our ominous and intimidating law enforcement and justice systems.

That is also what brought him to the National Motorists Association (NMA), of which he is now the California Chapter coordinator. The NMA is an organization that fights and lobbies for motorists' rights and interests. It has accomplished a great deal over the past decade. Most notable, and probably most familiar to you, was the institution of the 65 m.p.h. speed limit on many of our nation's freeways and rural highways. This happened almost completely as a result of this organization's efforts.

What I'm saying is that there are people out there who care about you, the motorist, and your rights. The author is one of them and he wrote this book for you.

Author's Note

This page is basically here to inform you that when this book was being written, the laws and codes were explained as they were understood at the time. The author is not a lawyer and therefore not licensed by anybody to give legal advice. This book is filled with suggestions, tactics, experiences and information designed to help you as much as possible, but in no way can they be construed as legal advice. You are probably well aware that laws are being changed, amended and distorted on a daily basis. So it is your responsibility to make a few phone calls, ask a few questions, find out if the laws are still the same, and which ones apply to you. They vary from one municipality to the next. This book is here to educate you on how to fight your ticket and explain your options. You, however, have to do the fighting.

There is a remote possibility that you can follow all the instructions and suggestions in this book and still not beat your ticket. "But why?" you scream in anguish. Because you might get a judge who decides you are guilty the minute you enter his courtroom because he doesn't like the way you walk. No matter what you do he will still find you guilty. (But then you *could* appeal and get a different judge.) In short, not the author, the publisher nor anyone quoted in this book can be held liable for your use of any of the information on these pages.

You *can* win – the odds are in your favor. After all, you are innocent until proven guilty.

Thanks

 Vola O'Shaughnessy (I spelled it right) For typing my first draft, sloppy handwritten mess that it was. (Boy that sure was a long time ago!)

 Patrick Naylor For giving me my title (even though he didn't know it) and some good advice and motivation for this book. P.S. Patrick: 10,000 copies is no problem.

 Franz Krachtus (my cartoonist) For some great drawings, and some good advice, too. If you like his work and want to get in touch with him, you can write him at P.O. Box 23646, Santa Barbara, CA 93121. By the way, Franz wants you to know: he has never received a ticket for a moving violation.

 **Julie Simpson** (& her computer) For putting the first edition together for me with her desktop publishing wizardry.

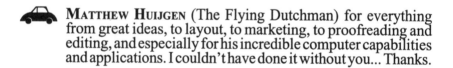 **James Ballantine** (and Peg Mowrer for recommending him) For all his help and suggestions.

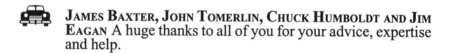 **Matthew Huijgen** (The Flying Dutchman) for everything from great ideas, to layout, to marketing, to proofreading and editing, and especially for his incredible computer capabilities and applications. I couldn't have done it without you... Thanks.

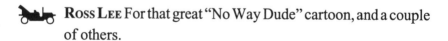 **James Baxter, John Tomerlin, Chuck Humboldt and Jim Eagan** A huge thanks to all of you for your advice, expertise and help.

Ross Lee For that great "No Way Dude" cartoon, and a couple of others.

Adryan Russ For a wonderful job of final editing. Thanks for getting it done so quickly on such short notice.

John and Susan Daniel For all your helpful hints, answers and contributions.

1

THE BEGINNING

Why Tickets Are Such A Huge Problem

There are nearly 100,000 tickets written in this country every day. Most of them are undeserved. Citations today are a large source of funding for most municipalities. Chicago, for example, brings in upwards of $100 million annually. Los Angeles, over $150 million; New York, in excess of $350 million. But they aren't the only ones cashing in. The insurance companies are also benefiting in a big way.

Consider that California issues about 10 million tickets annually. It is not uncommon for a person to end up paying nearly $1,000 in insurance surcharges over a three–year period, for just one ticket. This translates into a windfall that could reach $10 billion in California alone.

Also consider that numerous studies from very credible sources have demonstrated that a large number of tickets are completely unfounded and totally undeserved.

Yet about 90% of all Americans obediently mail in their fines unaware of what their contributions are promoting. They have a much better alternative: Taking a stand and fighting their tickets. Studies show that of all the people who challenge their citations, about half win. Considering the large sums of money at stake, it makes good sense to dispute a ticket.

The trouble is, most people don't realize how much they really end up paying for a ticket in the long run. Furthermore, they are intimidated by law enforcement and even more so by the court system. So even if they want to fight their citation, they often don't. Either they don't know where to start or they don't want to face the humiliation of going to court and being made to look like a fool. All they need is a little information and instruction and the whole picture changes.

That's what this book is all about. It not only goes through the whole citation process and breaks it down to its nuts and bolts, it also manages to keep a lighthearted sense of humor along the way. When you finish reading this book, you will know considerably more about tickets than most cops. This will give you the upper hand if you go to court. You will understand how the court system works. More importantly, you will understand how tickets don't work and therefore how to undermine, challenge and negate them. The strategies in this book work, and they can save you a tremendous amount of money.

Please understand that this book will not solve everyone's ticket woes. Example: You drink 17 bottles of JD, chase them with a keg of beer, hijack a rig and, without a license or insurance, run a bus–load of Jerry's kids of a one–lane bridge and only the bus driver lives to identify you. Guess what, buddy? You are in deep snow and the plow hasn't even been invented yet. In fact this book wouldn't want to have anything to do with helping you!

2

THE TICKET

What Is It And How Does It Work?

If you already know everything about tickets, you can skip this chapter. But if you already knew everything you wouldn't be reading this, would you?

A ticket is a little piece of paper that you get when you have allegedly violated a section of the vehicle code. There are two types of ticket violations. They are as different as night and day, and you need to know the difference. The two types are moving and non–moving violations. Tickets for moving violations, such as speeding, running a red light, illegal turn, etc., will hurt badly and quickly. Tickets for non–moving violations, such as parking and "fix it" tickets (brake light out), are trivial and will not harm you unless you totally ignore them.

Parking Tickets

If you get a parking ticket it will usually cost you a lot less in the long run if you just pay it. The time involved in fighting the ticket versus the cost of paying it, is hard to justify, unless you have nothing but time on your hands.

Repair Tickets

Repair tickets, or "fix its," as they are called, are very simple to deal with compared to most tickets. If you get a ticket for having a brake light out, fix the brake light. Any officer of the law will sign the back of the "fix it" ticket certifying that you repaired the violation in question. Then return the citation to the police agency that issued it. That's all there is to it.

Neither a parking nor a "fix it" ticket will ever appear on your driving record. However, if you ignore these tickets long enough you may face up to $500 in fines and six months in jail. The police agency will notify the court of your negligence, and the court will then issue a warrant for your arrest and charge you with either a "failure to appear" (FTA) and/or a failure to fix your violation.

Moving Violations

When you get a ticket for a moving violation, the process is a lot different than that of a "fix it" or parking ticket. When you sign the bottom of the ticket that the officer hands you, you are signing that you promise to appear in court on or before the date at the bottom of the ticket. If you do not sign the ticket, the police officer must arrest you and take you to jail. This seems to be a simple concept, but many people don't understand it. They think they are just signing for a received ticket. Then the ticket is thrown in the glove compartment, the court date deadline sneaks by, and guess what? They now have a failure to appear (FTA). Since this is a misdemeanor, a warrant is issued for their arrest, and the FTA appears on their driving record. If they're lucky, they will receive what is called a "courtesy notice" in the mail before their court date expires. It will give them the option of going to court as scheduled or paying an astronomical fine.

This is one of the biggest government rip–off scams in existence. Never, NEVER pay the "bail" on a courtesy notice instead of going to court. Here's why: If you go to court with absolutely no intention of fighting your ticket, the fine that the judge assesses will almost always be less than that of the bail on the courtesy notice. You save money no matter what. I received a courtesy notice on a speeding ticket once that had a bail amount of $300, and when I went to court I ended up paying only $70. It definitely pays to go to court. If you fight the ticket and win, you don't have to pay any fine and the ticket doesn't go on your driving record. If you pay the "bail" amount, it not only costs you a bundle, but it's treated as if you pleaded guilty and the ticket goes on your record. This in turn will raise your insurance rates, which will cost you a lot more than the ticket did. In other words, you lose twice.

```
SANTA BARBARA POLICE DEPARTMENT
NOTICE TO APPEAR                          No 217294
 □ TRAFFIC        □ OTHER
DATE              TIME         DAY      CASE NO.

NAME (FIRST, MIDDLE, LAST)

RESIDENCE ADDRESS      CITY      STATE        ZIP

BUSINESS ADDRESS       CITY      STATE        ZIP

DRIVER'S LICENSE NO.        STATE  CLASS SOC.SEC.#

SEX  RACE  HAIR   EYES    HEIGHT  WEIGHT  AGE  DATE OF BIRTH

VEHICLE LICENSE NO.       STATE  PHONE                C.V.
                                                   □ (V.C. 15210b)
YEAR VEH.  MAKE    MODEL    BODY STYLE  COLOR     □ H.M.(V.C. 353)

REGISTERED OWNER OR LESSEE                     □ SAME AS ABOVE
ADDRESS OF OWNER OR LESSEE                     □ SAME AS ABOVE
FINANCIAL RESPONSIBILITY

ELIGIBLE FOR DISMISSAL (V.C. 40610)
YES  NO   Violation(s)   Code     Description
□   □
□   □
□   □
□   □
    □  ALCOHOLIC BEVERAGE   DESCRIPTION
       DESTROYED AT SCENE
APPROX.  SAFE SPEED  SPEED LIMIT  RADAR . NUMBER  FORK   SURVEY DATE
                                 □YES
                                 □NO
LOCATION OF VIOLATION(S)
ON
WEATHER  STREET    TRAFFIC   DAWN       DIRECTION OF TRAVEL
CLEAR    DRY       LIGHT     DAY              N
FOG      SLIPPERY  MEDIUM    DUSK      W              E
RAIN     WET       HEAVY     NIGHT            S
I declare under penalty of perjury under the laws of the State of California that the foregoing is true and correct.
Date              Issuing Officer           I.D. No.
Division   Veh. No.              VACATION DATES:      TO
Name of arresting officer/citizen if different from above:
                                  I.D. No.
WITHOUT ADMITTING GUILT, I PROMISE TO APPEAR AT THE TIME AND PLACE CHECKED
BELOW. (See reverse for traffic bail and forfeiture information).
Signature X
   [  ]  IF CHECKED you must be fingerprinted PRIOR to your court date indicated
          below. Report to the Santa Barbara Police Department, 215 E. Figueroa St.,
          Monday-Friday, 8:00 A.M. - 12:00 P.M. only.
   [  ]  S, B, MUNICIPAL COURT    [  ] OTHER COURT _____
          118 E. Figueroa Street
          Santa Barbara, CA
on the _____ day of _____ , 19 ____
at _____ A.M.□  P.M.□  NIGHT COURT AVAILABLE □
   [  ]  PROBATION DEPARTMENT (Juvenile Misdemeanor Violations Only)
          Violator will be notified when/where to appear.
Form approved by the Judicial Council of California
(S) 3-11-91 v.c. 40513 (b), 40522, p.c. 853.5 SBPD No. 4.5 (15/93)
```

A typical ticket form. Notice where it says "Vacation Dates" a couple of lines above the signature line on the right side. The significance of this is explained at the beginning of Chapter 6 "How Do I Fight This Ticket?".

3

THE DMV AND
YOUR DRIVING RECORD

Getting Past The Red Tape

Your driving record is "maintained" by the Department of Motor Vehicles, or the DMV. Some states have slightly different names for this agency but they all perform the same function. If you have had any experience with the DMV, and of course you have, you know first hand what a seemingly hopeless mess of bureaucratic red tape it can be. Unfortunately, this institution has almost complete control over your driving record. They also have the power to issue, suspend and revoke your driver's license.

The DMV keeps track of your record using a point system. Each state has different point systems but they all operate pretty much the same way. The DMV keeps a running tab on your tickets and points and considers you a negligent driver if you exceed a certain number of points during a specified period of time. Most vehicle agencies keep traffic violations on your record for three years, although some keep them for as long as five years. At this point the violations drop off of your record and are no longer counted against you. The exception to this are drunk driving violations, which haunt you for seven years in most cases. If you rack up too many points the DMV will speedily send you a notice in the mail that your license is about to be suspended, which is exactly what will happen unless you quickly contact the DMV and make an appeal. If you do not call the DMV to request a hearing very shortly (usually within about 10 days) after receiving your suspension notice, you relinquish your right to do so. At this hearing you will need to present some evidence that your impending suspension is unjustified. This evidence can be an explanation of a ticket you didn't "deserve," in which case a witness is helpful, or you may plead your case for a restricted license instead of a suspended one. Basically, this means your license is only valid when you are driving to and from work or school. In any case, always give the hearing a shot because you have nothing to lose. They may suspend your license regardless, but if you have a good case, that's not likely.

Be sure to contact your local DMV and find out the exact numbers involved in their point system. Then you can keep track of your own record and avoid receiving a surprise license suspension in the mail one day. If you want to know how many points are now on your record, your local DMV will usually give you a printout of your driving record for a small charge.

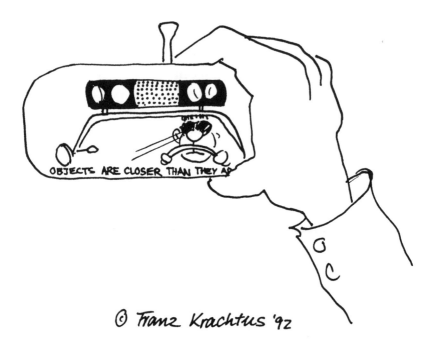

© Franz Krachtus '92

4

AVOIDING TICKETS

IN THE FIRST PLACE

Now that you have an idea of how tickets and the DMV function, let's talk about something far more important: How to avoid getting tickets in the first place.

Where Do They Come From?

Picture this: You are cruising down the freeway on a sunny Saturday afternoon with the flow of traffic, singing along with your favorite song and basically just having a great day. Suddenly these UFO's (unidentified flashing objects) appear in your rear view mirror and you're cursing under your breath, "Where the hell did he come from?"

If you read this book and only remember one thing, please remember this: PAY ATTENTION. Not only for your sake, but for the sake of everyone else on the road. You have mirrors and windows in your car for a reason. Use them. Here is another simple, logical concept that most people manage to ignore: If you are driving in a manner that might cause you to get a ticket, you should definitely be watching for cops.

There are several places where you should watch for cops. They like to play "hide and sneak." When you're on the freeway, you should always watch on-ramps. Many cops love to wait for speeders while sitting on an overpass. They then jump on the on-ramp merging in right behind them. This is known as the "swoop" maneuver. Always be wary of zipping by a pack of cars in front of you. They might be going slow because there is a squad car in front of them. Likewise, if you are watching your rear view mirror, which you should *always* be doing, and all those cars that were following right behind you suddenly slow way down, you might want to slow down too. There might be a trooper coming up behind them.

Always pass large trucks with caution because you can't see what's in front of them until you pass them. Cops know this and like to "hide" there. Watch for cops on freeways that have crossable center dividers. They like to sit in the middle and wait for you to go flying by. Elsewhere, on city streets, always be careful of hospital and school zones. Many officers sit and eat lunch in front of one of these two institutions because the speed limit is usually 25 m.p.h. or lower, and most people continue at the speed they were going the block before they got to the zone. Be careful going around blind corners, as well as at four-way stops, and of course around the police station.

Pay attention to what you are doing and always keep your eyes open for cops. The object is to spot them before they spot you.

Radar Detectors

While we are talking about avoiding tickets, let's talk about radar detectors. Basically, a radar detector is a radio that scans back and forth between several programmed frequencies. These frequencies are licensed to cops by the FCC (Federal Communications Commission) for radar enforcement.

Some detectors are not all they are cracked up to be and here's why. Most cops have radar units which they can turn on or off with a single switch. In order for these detectors to function, the radar must be on. If a cop waits until he sees you to turn on his radar, your detector will warn you too late.

Another disadvantage is that radar detectors can be very annoying in city traffic because so many security systems and alarms have frequencies near those of police radar. The result is that detectors constantly go off. Most are false warnings, so you can't tell what is a police warning and what isn't. There are a few sophisticated radar detectors on the market that have city/highway modes which allow you to screen out all the b.s. (that's bothersome sound). They also pick up intermittent radar, which means that if a cop is radaring individual cars and turning his unit on and off, your detector will pick that up and warn you in time to slow down. If, however, you are the only car on the road for miles – sorry! You don't get a warning. You get a ticket.

If you do a lot of speeding, purchasing a top-notch radar detector is highly recommended. It only has to save you from a ticket once to be worth the investment.

As far as recommendations, the Valentine detectors made by Valentine Research of Cincinnati, Ohio, have proven to be excellent units. For more information you can reach them at 1-800-331-3030.

Please note that Virginia and Washington D.C. have laws prohibiting the possession of a radar detector and fines of up to $5,000 for violators. New York and Illinois have similar regulations but they only apply to commercial vehicles. If you are in one of these states, be aware of these laws. Other states are currently working on legislation to restrict or ban radar detectors, so keep your eyes and ears open.

Drone Radar

A note for your information and personal enrichment: Several states are using what is called "Drone Radar" in various locations. It consists of little unmanned radar transmitters that never turn off. They are mounted in all sorts of creative locations near roads. The object is to fool people with radar detectors into slamming on their brakes and thus slowing down the speed of surrounding traffic. The problem is that they create road and traffic hazards in the process and certainly don't contribute to the smooth, efficient, safe flow of traffic.

5

WHEN YOU GET PULLED OVER

What To Say, What To Do

So you ignored the last chapter and didn't pay any attention to what you were doing and now the UFOs are in your rear view mirror. First of all, pull over to the side of the road as soon as possible. Make sure you do this in a safe manner and try to find a fairly safe parking place. Don't pull over in the middle of a bridge or a railway crossing. If you have something in the vehicle that you don't want to get caught with, it might be a good idea, after you pull over, to grab your license and registration and get out of your car. Do not, however, walk up to the patrol car. Just get away from yours. If you have nothing to hide, pull over, roll down your window and wait for the officer to approach. If it is nighttime, turn your dome light on. This makes it easier for the officer to see you. Do not make any quick or suspicious movements once you have been pulled over. These may alarm the officer or give him an excuse to search your vehicle. Keep your hands on the steering wheel so the officer can see them. The best thing to do is to wait until he reaches your window and asks you for your license and registration before you make any kind of movement whatsoever. A "routine" traffic stop is always potentially dangerous for an officer. He doesn't know if you're an escaped convict with an AK47 or not. The officer is taking his life into his hands. Don't give him any reason to fear for it.

Here's a special note for you lucky folks who live in one of the 40+ states that currently have seatbelt laws: If you have your seat belt on, leave it on, but if you don't, do not try to "sneak" it on. This is very obvious and it really irritates cops because they often take it as an insult.

Always let the officer do the talking and, when you answer

his questions, make your replies brief and non–incriminating. If you are being pulled over for speeding and the officer asks you how fast you were going, your reply should always be something like; "You know, I'm not really sure" or "Gosh, I really don't know," or something else non–incriminating. What he is trying to do is get you to incriminate yourself. Don't fall for it. Be as polite as you possibly can to the officer at all times. You never know how many times he's been shot at that day and what kind of mood he's in. The majority of the traffic cops out there are human, regardless of what you may think. If you are courteous to them they are likely to be courteous to you.

If he asks if he can search your vehicle or says, "Mind if I look around?" politely tell him that he may not search your car. An officer cannot search your vehicle without "probable cause," a warrant, or your permission. In order to have "probable cause" an officer must have a good indication that you are hiding something illegal. Perhaps he observed you stuffing something under the seat as he approached your car, or your car and/or your breath smell like weed, or booze.

If he says he can get a warrant, invite him to go ahead. If he has to ask your permission to search your car, he doesn't have probable cause. Without that a judge won't give him a warrant. If you do let him search your vehicle, you are taking a couple of risks: First, a lot of people have no idea what is legal or illegal to have in their cars. You might get busted for something you had no idea was against the law to have in your car. Second, a search gives a cop the chance to plant incriminating evidence if he is so inclined. The choice is yours, but you have the right to say no.

Searches aside, if you are dealing with a somewhat "cool" cop, you may want to ask him some questions relative to the violation he is citing you for. For example "How far away from me were you when you observed the **alleged** violation?" If nighttime, "Did you have your lights on?" If a speeding violation, "How did you determine my speed?" If radar, "May I take a look at the readout on the radar unit?"

Be careful when questioning the officer who stops you not to

phrase a question like this: "Where were you when I ran the stop sign?" This is admitting guilt and kills any chance you might have of fighting the ticket in court. This is why the use of the word "alleged" was emphasized in the first sample question.

Once again, always remember to be as polite as you possibly can. After the officer has given you your ticket and retreated to his car, make a few notes about the situation. What agency was the officer from? What was his name? All officers have name tags pinned to their chest. What did he or she look like? Also, note where you are, where the alleged violation occurred, whether the traffic is light or heavy, what the weather is like and anything else you think may be useful information in court. By doing this, you give the officer time to pull out first. Although a cop is not likely to give you two separate tickets in a row, it is always safer to have a cop in front of you than behind you, and it definitely makes you a little less nervous.

6

How Do I Fight This Ticket?

The Options, The Strategies, And More

One of the most important things to remember in fighting your ticket is that if you are present in court on your trial date and the police officer who ticketed you does not show up, your ticket will be dismissed right then and there for "lack of prosecution." Sometimes you must ask for this dismissal but usually not.

Why wouldn't the police officer show up? There are lots of reasons. He may have an important meeting. There may be an emergency, or he might even be on vacation. Any time someone challenges a citation, the issuing officer is always notified because he or she must be present at the trial as the state's witness. There are a couple of ways that you can make it more difficult for the officer to make it to the trial. First of all, some states have a little known option that allows you to request that the trial be held at the "county seat," if you live or work closer to the county seat than the court the officer puts on the back of your ticket as your place to appear. The county seat is basically the capitol of your county and always has a municipal or justice court. This request is nothing more than a "change of venue," something that occurs frequently in criminal cases.

The advantages of doing this are several. First, the officer is less likely to show up for the trial because the county seat might be a long way from his home base. Second, he probably won't know the judge, as opposed to his home court where he probably knows and has worked and played with all of the judges. Third, the ticket might get lost because county seat requests are very unusual. However, you must request the county seat when the officer issues you the ticket. Otherwise he will write the court that is closest to his home base as the place to appear, and that is where the ticket will be sent. If the officer refuses your request, go ahead and sign the ticket but write somewhere on the ticket that you requested the county seat as the place to appear but were refused (before he tears the ticket out of his book so your note shows up on his copy) The problem is that many cops have never heard of this and may think you are giving them some kind of bogus b.s., but it is your legal right. You can get the case transferred later when you are dealing with a person more knowledgeable than a traffic cop. You must, however, have proof that you made the request and it was refused. You, of course, may get a ticket in or close to the county seat – or in a county that has only one court, the court at the county seat – in which case requesting the county seat would not only be futile, but would make you look really stupid.

Another way you can make showing up more difficult on a cop is to find out when his vacation is and try to schedule your trial so it falls during his vacation. Many times you don't have to look any further than your ticket to find out when his vacation is. There is a place on many citation forms for him to fill in when it is, so the court clerks won't schedule any trials during that time period. However, most of the time clerks don't even read this part, so if you call the court and request an extension to a date that just "happens" to be during the officer's vacation, chances are they will grant it to you, no problem. Incidentally, in most municipalities you are usually allowed one extension over the phone, up to a maximum of 30 days. After that, you must show up in court to request another extension, which is usually granted, provided you come up with a good reason. It is usually a good idea to take a couple of extensions. The longer the time period between the citation and the trial, the more the officer is likely to forget about the details surrounding the ticket. After all, he writes hundreds of them and doesn't have an elephant's memory.

...HOW DO YOU PLEAD TO THE CHARGE OF SPEEDING?

Speeding Violations

A Note About The 55 m.p.h. Speed Limit

On the subject of speeding, here is some important information on the 55 m.p.h. speed limit. Some of you may know this and some of you may not, but the reason that we have the 55 m.p.h. speed limit has absolutely nothing to do with "saving lives." That's just what the government wants you to believe. The national maximum speed limit law was passed in 1974 by the Nixon administration and its sole purpose was to conserve fuel. It is a fact that driving "55" saves fuel. If you remember back to 1974, we were in the midst of an alleged fuel shortage. But guess what folks? THE CRISIS IS OVER and 20 years later we still have the 55 m.p.h. speed limit.

The reason the government wants you to believe that "55 saves lives" is that you will think we have the law for a good reason. The real reason we still have the 55 m.p.h. speed limit is because it provides the government (and insurance companies) with a huge revenue source: speeding tickets. They know that most people don't obey the law, but they keep it because it brings in revenue. So just how big is the ticket business? Well, between the tickets themselves and the resulting insurance company surcharges, we are talking about hundreds of billions of dollars.

Okay, maybe you are saying "Yeah, but don't speeders get in more accidents?" A recent Federal Highway Administration (FHA) study by transportation engineers Samuel C. Tignor and Davey Warren concluded just the opposite. Of all the drivers studied, the slowest 5% of these had the highest accident rate. Does that surprise you? It shouldn't.

Guess what else they found. Those drivers whose speeds were 10–15 m.p.h. ABOVE the speed limit had the lowest accident rate. Think about that for a minute. That means that you are SAFER exceeding our current speed limit than obeying it. If

you don't believe it, you're the unfortunate victim of brainwashing. Think about it this way. Slow drivers are less attentive than faster drivers. That's why they drive slowly. Tourists are a great example of this. Unfortunately for slow drivers, their slowness doesn't save them. Statistics show that more than HALF of all accidents are due to inattentive drivers.

Returning to the FHA study, Tignor and Warren also found that 70% of all motorists exceed the speed limit and that most speed limits are set at least 10 m.p.h. below the average speed of traffic.

The 85th Percentile Rule

Let's talk about the "average speed of traffic" for a minute. Most of you are familiar with this speed. It's the speed at which you usually drive. Another way to look at this is "going with the flow" of traffic. There have been studies upon studies done that show most people drive at a speed which is prudent and safe under current conditions, regardless of the speed limit. From these studies has come the 85th percentile rule. It states that the safest speed is the speed that 85% of the people travel at or below, under normal conditions, on a given road. It is with this rule that traffic engineers set speed limits. Unless, of course, they are prevented from doing so by some stupid law, politician, or special interest group. This, by the way, is the case most of the time.

My guess is that at least once in your life you, or at least someone you know, have been picked out of a group of cars all traveling along at the same <u>safe</u> speed and given a speeding ticket. You likely complained (and rightfully so), "But officer, I was going with the flow of traffic." His reply was probably something like, "That's no excuse to break the law."

Let's go back to the FHA study one more time. Why do you suppose that the drivers whose speeds were 10–15 m.p.h. above the speed limit had the lowest accident rate? Does it not stand to reason that if you are going with the flow of traffic, you are safer than if you are not? If 70% of all motorists exceed the speed limit by at least 10 m.p.h. then they <u>are</u> the flow of traffic and they <u>are</u>

traveling at the safest speed and they <u>will</u> have the lowest accident rate.

Do you see what a gold mine this is for municipalities and insurance companies?

If speed limits are raised, people will continue to drive as they always have. The only difference is that they won't be breaking the law anymore. Accident rates will go down because many of the people who currently obey the speed limits will join the flow of traffic, reducing the number of slow–moving hazards on the road.

The American Association of State Highway and Transportation Officials (AASHTO) recently sent the following policy resolution to Congress, state governors and the FHA. They stated: "Implementation of the National Maximum Speed Limit has created confusion and has generated considerable criticism due to unexpected and apparently unnecessary speed limit reductions. Motorists have clearly demonstrated through their actions that they believe arbitrary speed limits to be unreasonable. Now, therefore be it resolved that the Board of Directors of AASHTO urges Congress to allow the states to set reasonable speed limits on urban and rural highways following established traffic engineering principles."

The reason the 55 m.p.h. speed limit is being blasted is because it is obviously a useless law. The reason you have been given all this information that isn't directly related to actually fighting your ticket is because it is important to use this book to fight <u>ALL</u> your speeding tickets, not just the ones you suspect you're not guilty of. Even if you are technically guilty, please understand that, in most cases, you are not guilty at all. There's little doubt that you were driving at a safe and sane speed.

Radar

Of all moving violations that are issued, the majority of these are speeding tickets. A large number of speeding tickets are now radar enforced. For some strange reason radar is an incredibly ominous word to some people. They think they are defenseless against a radar enforced speeding ticket. Everybody thinks radar is infallible because it is digital and computerized. Nothing could be further from the truth. There are many, many factors that can cause a radar reading to be inaccurate; and if you can prove or even raise a suspicion that any of these factors were involved in your radar speeding ticket, you have a good chance of getting your ticket dismissed.

Let's examine how radar works so you will have some understanding of how it can easily be inaccurate. When a radar unit is pointed at you and activated, it emits radio waves at a certain frequency which travel to your vehicle, bounce off of it and return to the radar unit at a different frequency. This different frequency is gauged entirely on how fast you are going. The radar unit then measures the difference between the two frequencies, outgoing and incoming, and converts that calculation to a miles–per–hour speed. Sounds simple, right? Sometimes. The radar unit, to get a correct reading, must be pointed straight at you to read your speed.

Plus there can't be any obstruction in the way. Furthermore, the unit must be fairly close to you to insure that it is not reading another vehicle's speed in another lane. A radar unit does not emit a straight, tight beam; instead, its beam is just like that of a flashlight. In other words, the farther the beam travels, the more it spreads out: Thus, the room for error is increased. At a distance of merely one–eighth of a mile from the unit, a radar beam is four lanes wide. So if you get a radar speeding ticket, ask the officer how far away you were when he "clocked" you. If this distance was great enough, he may have even clocked someone in the far lane on the other side of the road.

Radar also has a tendency to read speeds of larger objects over smaller ones. Example: You are in the right lane of the road and there is a large truck coming up behind you in the left lane. A police officer with a radar unit points it at you and gets a speed reading of 72 m.p.h., quite a bit faster than you were actually going. What really happened is that the radar unit read the large truck's speed but the officer attributed the speed to you because you were in front.

Radar can also be affected by rain and blowing objects, because it measures the speed of anything that moves. Believe it or not, the speed of blowing dust, leaves or branches that the radar unit reads can accidentally be attributed to you. If you get a radar speeding ticket under windy or stormy conditions, you might have a good argument for dismissal of the ticket.

A note about the hand–held radar "guns" commonly used by motorcycle cops: When a cop with a radar gun stations himself along a road with the intention of ticketing speeders, he may keep the gun down at his side in an effort to conceal it. Then he'll raise it quickly in order to get a speed reading before you react and slow down. The problem with this is that when the officer raises the gun quickly, the unit not only measures your speed but it adds the speed of the officer's arm motion. This can increase the speed reading by eight to ten m.p.h.! Keep your eyes open for cops with radar guns and pay attention to how they handle them. An officer's arm speed might be grounds for a speeding ticket dismissal in court.

If you get a radar enforced ticket for breaking a posted speed limit (anything less than the maximum speed limit), this little tidbit could be very useful to you: In some places a police officer cannot use radar to enforce speeding tickets if a "traffic and engineering survey" has not been conducted and maintained on the road where he is using radar for this purpose. Such a survey determines the 85th percentile speed on a certain road. It is from these surveys that most posted speed limits are supposed to be set.

These "traffic and engineering surveys" must be updated, usually every five years, in order for radar to be used legally for enforcing speeding tickets. This is important because if you get a radar enforced speeding ticket, the officer must bring a certified copy of an up–to–date "traffic and engineering survey" to court with him. This survey must have been performed on the roadway where he gave you the citation. If the officer does not do this, the judge will usually dismiss the case. A lot of judges do not ask for this document from the officer, so many times cops don't bring them, or they just plain don't exist. Therefore it is up to you to make this request. If you would like to obtain the survey before-hand so you can check it over, ask for it at the engineering department of your local city hall. Some judges in California now allow you to also request the actual data that made up the survey. This allows you to challenge the accuracy of the survey itself.

Many surveys are conducted with one of these devices shown in the photo on the right. They are stationary radar units with large digital display screens. These screens tell oncoming drivers how fast they are going. The problem is that most people slam on their brakes when they see one of these things. They are afraid some cop is going to jump out from behind the thing and give them a ticket. This, of course, distorts the survey and gives a lower 85th percentile speed, from which they can "justifiably" set a lower speed limit. So when you see one of these things, hit the other pedal.

A large number of radar enforced speeding citations are dismissed every year because the defendant asks for any or all of the following items and doesn't get them:

1. The radar unit's calibration and maintenance records.

2. The officer's radar training certification(s).

3. The tuning fork(s) used to calibrate the radar unit and their calibration certificates.

4. The actual radar unit that was used.

5. The agency's FCC (Federal Communications Commission) license.

6. List of models, makes and serial numbers of all radar units being used by that agency.

Here's how the procedure works. Every state in this country has a public records law that allows the public access to certain records. You have two possible options when requesting this "stuff."

First, you can go directly to the issuing officer's agency and ask to speak to the public records custodian or officer. You then present them with a list of what you want. If they cooperate, they will probably give you everything they have except for the radar unit itself and the tuning forks. Most likely they will inform you that the officer will bring these with him on your trial date. They generally don't pass out radar units and forks to anyone who walks in and asks for them. If they do not cooperate, you have two more options. You can call the state attorney general, who prosecutes all violations of the public records law. You can bet you'll get your records really fast, if they have them, after the attorney general gives them a call. Or you may be really vindictive and decide to file a civil lawsuit against the agency for punitive damages. You are entitled to them in this instance.

Second, you can subpoena the items from the court. Make your request to the court clerk explaining exactly what it is you want. When using a subpoena, you need to give the court at least two weeks notice before your trial date. The only drawback to using subpoenas is that you usually don't get to inspect the "goodies" until you actually get to court.

In any case, if you try and do not get all, or any, of the items requested, you have a very good chance of getting your case dismissed.

When you get all of this "stuff," look at it carefully and see if you can use it to your advantage in court. First, look to see that everything is up to date and accurate. If it's not, that's almost as good as not getting it at all. The absence or inaccuracy of the radar unit's calibration and maintenance records, the tuning forks's calibration certificate(s) or the officer's radar training certificate(s) make excellent courtroom ammunition for you. They leave the officer very shaky ground upon which to testify.

Every law enforcement agency that uses radar must have a license from the FCC to do so. If it doesn't, not only is your ticket history, but the agency is in big trouble. This scenario, however, is very unlikely.

On the FCC license will be a list of the models, makes and serial numbers of all radar units that a particular agency is licensed to use. Agencies are frequently acquiring new radar units. Sometimes they fail to register these with the FCC. These units are therefore unlicensed. When you finally get to check out the radar unit, make sure its serial number is listed on that agency's license. If it is not, they can't use it against you in court.

There are several things that can cause unintentional false

speed readings on radar units.

These can all be additional "artillery" in court:

●※A radar unit can sometimes read the speed of a patrol car's heater or air conditioner fan.

●※An inadvertent false reading can appear on a radar unit if the unit's antenna (which is moveable) is pointed, even briefly, at the readout part of the unit.

●※Neon lights, power transformers and lines, electrical storms and other sources of harmonic frequencies can all influence radar readings.

●※Radio transmitters and towers are great sources of radar interference. After all, radar itself is a radio wave. Citizen's Band (CB) radios are especially inclined to distort radar unit speed readings. In fact many officers have CBs in their cars, making this interference a frequent occurrence.

●※Moving radar, which is no different from stationary radar, other than the fact that it must figure the patrol car's speed into the equation, can be guilty of what is known as "batching." This occurs when the officer accelerates too quickly. The radar unit will not immediately adjust for the officer's sudden increase in ground speed. Until it does, it will add the officer's increase in speed to the speed of the target–you. This can easily produce a substantial error, provide a completely inaccurate reading, and lead to an unwarranted citation.

Here is one more scenario that can happen. You could be traveling down a road approaching a lower speed zone. An officer could clock you from a considerable distance away. By the time your speed gets back to his unit you have entered the lower speed zone. Even though you have since slowed down, his unit is showing your former speed and he reads it as the speed you are currently traveling in the lower speed zone.

Laser (Lidar)

Chances are that by now you've heard of laser, but you may still not know much about it. The reason for that is because its use has not been very widespread. That seems to be changing. Laser is a speed–measuring device that uses a laser beam, instead of the radio wave beam radar uses. It is also referred to as "lidar" which stands for LIght Detection And Ranging. It has a very tight straight–line beam, unlike radar's flashlight beam. This, of course, makes it far more selective in pinpointing targets than radar, which is bad news for you. Lidar also renders your radar detector completely useless. More bad news for you.

But there is good news. First, lidar guns are far more tricky to operate than their radar counterparts, making them not terribly popular with many cops. Second, if you own a black Corvette or RX7 you have little to worry about. What am I talking about? Well, since lidar uses light to measure speed, there has to be something on your car to reflect the light back to the lidar gun so it can complete the speed calculation. If your vehicle deflects all of the light the lidar gun sends out, the speed reading will be blank. So if you have a dark colored vehicle with retracting headlights and virtually no chrome (a black Corvette), it will be almost impossible for a lidar gun to obtain a speed reading on you. The only target the cop will have left is your front license plate. By tilting your plate upward a bit, you can make it deflect the laser signal instead of reflect it.

So there you have it. You've been wanting a new 'vette, or RX7, or 300ZX anyway, haven't you? Well, now you have a great excuse to buy one... They're virtually immune to lidar. If your budget can't accommodate that kind of extravagance, some headlight covers and a bra will greatly increase your chances of sneaking by a lidar gun undetected. One of the main keys, as I mentioned before, in avoiding lidar detection is deflecting, instead of reflecting, the laser signal. In other words, the more sleek, aerodynamic and angular your vehicle, the better. Big trucks and vans are sitting ducks for cops with lidar guns.

Some people claim very powerful driving lights can overwhelm a laser signal. And, if you hadn't guessed, there are companies already cranking out lidar detectors. (Probably the same companies that make lidar guns. What a great business!)

© Franz Krachtus '92

GUESS WHAT, YOU MADE
ME SPILL MY COFFEE!

Pacing

There are several other methods an officer can use to determine your speed. The next most commonly used method is "pacing." All this means is that the officer follows you for a while traveling at the same speed you are and thus determines your speed. He may pace you for a quarter of a mile, and then again he may be bored and pace you for 10 miles. In fact all he has to do legally is match your speed. Whichever he does, he can still gauge how fast you are going.

One possible attack on pacing is to ask the officer the last time his speedometer was calibrated. You should probably try to obtain as much of his vehicle's calibration records as you can before you get to court. Follow the same procedures outlined earlier for obtaining radar related documentation. Look everything over carefully for any discrepancies, inaccuracies and especially for any records of his speedometer being off by a substantial amount. This will establish a history of inaccuracy on the part of his speedometer.

When you get to court, don't tell him you have his records. Ask him about them and see if he contradicts them. He almost certainly won't bring them. He also probably won't remember the details of what's on them and may try to ad lib to save his credibility. You may get the opportunity to really embarrass him. In any case, if it's been a while since his vehicle has been calibrated and it has a sketchy history, you can raise a lot of doubt regarding the accuracy of your citation.

Now an important note: An officer can pace you just as easily while he's ahead of you as he can when he's behind you. I am not trying to make you feel stupid, but I learned this the hard way. I was cruising down the freeway once at about 70 m.p.h. in the fast lane and noticed a highway patrol officer a ways back in my rearview mirror. Naturally I slowed down and moved over into the center lane. He proceeded to blow right by me. Figuring he was on call or chasing someone else, I resumed my original speed in the far lane. A couple of minutes later he pulled over to the shoulder allowing me to pass him. He then caught up to me, pulled me over and wrote me a speeding ticket claiming that he paced me while he was in front of me. So don't make the same mistake.

Visual Estimation & VASCAR

There are two more ways cops measure speed. The first one is by means of visual estimation. This is just a euphemism for "guessing." Here is a wonderful courtroom demonstration that can make an officer look really silly in some cases. Suppose you're in court for a speeding violation. At some point the officer may testify what he estimated your speed to be. In your rebuttal, challenge his ability to estimate speed. Take any object, hold it shoulder high, and drop it. Then ask: "Officer, could you estimate how fast this object was traveling when it hit the ground?" You will already know the answer. All objects fall at the same rate regardless of weight. All you have to do is measure the distance from your shoulder to the ground.

Below is a table for you. It shows a distance in feet on one side. You will want this distance to match up to your shoulder height. On the other side it shows the speed that an object will be traveling when it hits the ground after being dropped from that height.

Table	
Distance (in feet)	**m.p.h.** (rounded to one decimal)
3.5	10.2
4.0	10.9
4.5	11.6
5.0	12.2
5.5	12.8
6.0	13.4
6.5	13.9

Let's say you dropped your object from 5–1/2 feet. And let's say the officer's guess is 15 m.p.h., off by about 2 m.p.h. If your citation was for 60 m.p.h., then the officer's visual estimation would have been off by about 10 m.p.h. His margin of error will increase as the speed increases. In this case the speed was increased 5–fold, from 12 to 60 m.p.h. Therefore the margin of error would also increase 5–fold, from 2 to 10 m.p.h.

Needless to say, cops try not to write too many tickets based on this method of speed measurement alone because it is difficult to prove.

The last method of speed calculation used is called VASCAR, which stands for Visual Average Speed Computer And Recorder. Here's how it works: An officer decides on a beginning and an ending point on a given road. He then measures the distance between these two points. Next, he waits for you to cross the beginning point and starts his stopwatch. When you reach the ending point the police officer stops his watch and enters your "time" in the computer, which in turn tells him how fast you were going. If you remember way back to pre–algebra, speed equals time divided by distance. Anyway, that's all the computer is calculating. The trouble with this method is that if the officer misjudges when you cross his "lines" and starts his timer late and/ or stops it early, your speed gets calculated higher than it actually was. For this reason the use of VASCAR has been outlawed in some places because it can be used as a "speed trap."

VASCAR is a very accurate method of determining speed as long as the officer doesn't cheat. It can be used other ways too. Example: A trooper passes you on the freeway. As he passes you he starts measuring distance and time. Then he sails off into the sunset at some exorbitant speed, still measuring distance and time. You figure he's on a call and resume your previous behavior. Five miles down the road he stops measuring distance and pulls over. He waits for you to cross the five–mile line and then stops measuring time. He now has the time that it took you to travel the past five miles. He divides five miles into your time and... abracadabra... he's got your speed! The officer can also do what amounts to the inverse of this operation if you are traveling in the opposite direction, although admittedly it's a bit more difficult.

Especially if he decides to turn around and go chase you after completing his calculation.

Air Patrolling

This may be news to you, and then again it may not. There are quite a few speeding citations issued by, or actually instigated by, highway patrolmen in airplanes. Haven't you ever seen one of those signs "Patrolled by Aircraft?" They're not kidding. The reason this is mentioned now is because air patrolmen often use the VASCAR method of determining speed. If VASCAR is illegal in their state, they supposedly obtain the pace of the car from the plane and use that as their evidence. Yeah, right. What do they think we are, stupid? Airspeed and groundspeed are two totally different measurements. Anyway, when they "clock" someone exceeding the speed limit, they radio down to a patrolman on the ground with a description of the offending vehicle. The ground patrolman will then try to locate the vehicle, based on the description he was given. If he spots the described "speeder" he will then try to pace the vehicle himself so he doesn't have to rely solely on the testimony of his compadre in the sky. However, many times the "speeder" will see him coming and slow down, making it impossible for the officer to obtain a pace of this driver. Nevertheless the alleged speeder usually gets a ticket.

As you can already see, this operation has lots of "holes" in it. Besides the possible inaccuracy of the VASCAR measurement and, need we even say, the pace, how in the world is the officer on the ground supposed to be sure he has the right vehicle?

To illustrate the point, let's say you drive a black pickup. As you well know, there are lots of black, not to mention dark colored, pickups on the road. Since the air patrolman cannot possibly read your license plate number from his vantage point, all the officer on the ground has to go on is a general description of what your car looks like. Unless he actually obtains his own speed reading of your vehicle, he really has no solid evidence to prosecute you with. Furthermore, when you challenge one of these tickets, both the patrolman in the airplane and the officer on the ground must show

up in court because both of their testimonies are necessary to have a case against you. This of course doubles your chances of winning by default since there are two officers that have to show up instead of one. If both of them do show up, make sure that when they take the stand, you have the judge ask each of them to leave the room while the other is testifying. This will prevent them from prompting each other. It will also increase the chances of them contradicting each other. If their stories don't jive, it makes them look really bad, and your case much better. Anyway you get the idea. If you ever get one of these tickets, please fight it. They are almost impossible to lose.

Photo Radar

And you thought we were finished with radar? Not quite. If "cops in planes" was shocking news to you, photo radar will be even more shocking. I would like to start off by sharing a true story with you. Recently a lady was opening her mail when she came across an official looking envelope. Inside, she was greeted by a ticket that was attributed to her and her husband's car. But that wasn't all she found. Along with the ticket, there were a couple of photos of the car enclosed, one of which showed her husband and an unidentified female "companion" frolicking in the front seat. To make a long story short: The couple ended up splitting and the husband sued the state for invasion of privacy.

Now, some of you might be saying: "Well, that serves him right." The rest of you are saying: "Boy, I hope that never happens to me." Either way it doesn't matter because my point is not about "cheating on your spouse," it is about invasion of your right to privacy.

First, however, let's examine photo radar and how it works. A photo radar unit is exactly what it sounds like: a radar unit with a camera and a computer attached to it. The computer is programmed to signal the camera to take a picture of any vehicle clocked exceeding a certain speed. The photo is taken of the front of the car as it is important to get the driver's face in the picture. In some cases there will be two cameras. This makes it possible to get a picture of the rear of the car. States that do not require front license plates use this setup, so they can get a photo of the rear license plate. All of this happens as you unsuspectingly drive by the photo radar unit. At the end of the day or week the photos with legible license plate numbers are sorted out. The license numbers are then fed into the computer and tickets are mailed out to the corresponding registered owners.

Sounds pretty scary, doesn't it? It actually gets a bit worse. Similar units are being installed at selected stoplights around the country. The difference is that instead of radar, these units have sensors at the limit lines of the intersection. If a vehicle crosses the limit line, even just a little bit, while the light is red, its picture is taken and its owner is mailed a ticket.

All right, now that you know how photo radar is supposed to function please allow me to gleefully blow some gaping holes in it. If you ever receive a photo radar ticket, my first suggestion would be to ignore it. You can even throw the damn thing in the trash can, or use it for kindling or maybe even line your bird cage with it. The chances of you ever hearing another word about it are next to nothing. Here's why.

When you receive a normal ticket from a cop, you sign the bottom of the citation promising to appear. When you get a photo radar ticket you never sign anything. Legally you don't have to respond, appear, pay, or anything else. The only way you'll ever hear anything about it is if an officer shows up at your door with a court summons. When he asks you about the ticket you might reply: "I'm sorry, officer, I never received a ticket, it must have been lost in the mail." Since they don't send these tickets out via "certified" mail, there's no way to prove you received it. But you'll probably never need to. Photo radar is a business. They'd never make any money if they had to pay summons servers to come to your door. They just bank on a certain number of obedient, ignorant people mailing in their fines. This is also true for citations that are issued in conjunction with a collision. If the collision was your fault, you will often be sent a ticket in the mail. Once again you never signed it. They don't send these out registered mail either. However, if you choose to ignore one of these, there will usually be a warrant issued for your arrest. If and when they do catch up with you and arrest you, you have the right to sue the county or appropriate municipality for pain and suffering, loss of wages etc., if you are so inclined.

If you do decide to challenge your photo radar ticket, the most important thing is to request to see the picture(s). You might get them in the mail along with your notice but that's not likely. They learned after being sued for invasion of privacy.

Statistics indicate that the vast majority of photo radar pictures are illegible in at least one of the three critical categories:

1. Legible license plate number.

2. Make and model of the car identifiable.

3. Distinguishable driver.

The latter, number 3, is usually unclear. One defendant reportedly told a judge, "I don't know who that is, your Honor, but it sure isn't me." The judge replied, "You mean to tell me this is your car and you don't know who is driving it?" "That's right, your Honor. Everyone in the family has the keys to the car and they've always let their friends drive it too." It's unlikely the judge subpoenaed their whole family.

In order for a photo radar ticket to make it to your mail box, your license plate number has to be legible in the pictures. How else could they find your address? I can hear them in the sorting room: "Hey Sarg, you know this guy?" "Yeah, that's my mechanic. I'll go look his address up for you right now." Anyway, the object is to make your plates as obscure to the cameras as possible. If you live in a state that requires front plates, you can remove your front license plate. It serves no purpose anyway, which is demonstrated by the fact that a large number of states do not require front plates. Please be aware that, although unlikely, you may receive a citation for not having a front plate if your state requires it. This is, however, only a repair violation. You can fix and unfix this quickly and easily. Another good stealth tactic is to throw gobs of mud on your license plate. Warning! Your vehicle has to be just as muddy or you will look suspicious. You subject yourself to another kind of ticket if the plate is too illegible. If you have a truck, leave your tailgate down. It obstructs the view of the license plate. You get the added benefit of better gas mileage due to the reduced resistance.

Many people have had success painting their plates with a high gloss coat. This often causes them to glare in a photo but the plates are still readable with the naked eye. Two dollars for a can of high gloss coat and two minutes of your time are all you need. If your municipality uses photo radar (just look for the signs saying "Speed Enforced by Photo Radar"), this operation might be a worthwhile investment.

Here's a little background information and commentary on photo radar that you will probably find interesting. You probably think that photo radar units are owned by the police or the highway patrol. Think again. Most of these machines are owned and operated by private companies. That's right – private companies! Since most local municipalities cannot afford these expensive beasts, they instead lease them from private companies. These companies "maintain" the photo radar units and send the municipality a percentage of the loot (fees collected). So you see, this is revenue generation, or taxation as we know it, in its purest form. Nowhere is there any intent to improve public safety or protect anybody, which is what law enforcement is supposed to do. Consider this: If a drunk driver is speeding and swerving all over the road and passes a photo radar unit, what happens? Answer: He gets a speeding ticket in the mail after he is involved in a fatal accident that leaves two children dead. Did the photo radar machine do any good? You think about it!

Radar Cheating

Now this may be hard to believe, but just as there are dishonest people, history has shown us that there are dishonest cops. When quota time approaches, some cops are very capable of cheating on your ticket, specifically with a false radar reading. Although "quotas," as they are called, were officially outlawed many years ago, they still exist in an unwritten form in many places. Actually that's not entirely true. In Missouri and Illinois citation quotas are still used in progress evaluations of police officers. A quota is simply the quantity of tickets an officer is expected to issue over a certain period of time. If he issues a lot fewer tickets than that, he may get passed over for a raise or a promotion. So, although quotas may not actually exist on paper, they do exist in the back of an officer's head. If he is getting behind he just might resort to cheating.

How does he do that? Well, when radar is involved there are several possibilities. An officer can clock someone else's speed, show it to you and say it is yours. If an officer has a CB in his car, he can whistle into the microphone and cause his radar unit to read almost any speed he wants. The speed reading depends upon, and increases with, the pitch of his whistle. He can also obtain a false reading by aiming the radar unit at the ground and swinging it in an arc which the unit reads as a certain speed. An experienced cop can get the unit to read almost any speed he wants. Another possible method of obtaining a false reading is clocking a low flying aircraft, and believe it or not, officers have reportedly done just that. If an officer has a car–mounted radar unit he can get a false reading by simply turning the unit to "calibrate mode," in which state the unit will display whatever speed the officer is calibrating. The calibrate mode is designed to help the officer check the accuracy of his radar unit at different speeds. In other words, it is an equipment testing device. But if he is desperate to write a ticket, he may use the calibrate mode to "prove" to you how fast you were going.

© Franz Krachtus '92

If you are pulled over for a speeding ticket, always ask the officer if he used radar and if so, could you take a look at the reading on the unit. If he says no, be very suspicious and definitely fight that ticket. If he says sure, look to see if the switch on the unit is turned to calibrate mode. If it is, chances are this guy is cheating and you should still take him to court. While you're at it, ask him if you can see his tuning fork. As far as the courts are concerned, tuning forks are the only acceptable test of the radar unit's accuracy. The forks come in many different speed denominations. For example, let's say an officer has a 65 m.p.h. fork. When he holds it up to the radar unit and strikes it, the unit should read a speed of 65 m.p.h. If he were so inclined, he could turn around and use this reading as evidence for a false speeding citation. According to most law enforcement agency procedure manuals, a cop is supposed to calibrate his unit with a tuning fork before and after each violation and at the beginning and end of his shift. If he can't show you his fork, he's probably not doing his job. This is good ammunition in court. It's usually not enough to get a dismissal by itself, but it sure helps. It makes it impossible for him to establish beyond a reasonable doubt that his unit was functioning correctly at the time he cited you.

This is why, as mentioned earlier, it is a good idea to obtain the radar unit's calibration records as well as the tuning fork's calibration certificates. If there are any weak or missing points, you can attack them.

Speeding Legally

This may sound hard to believe, but besides speeding to the delivery room with a pregnant lady in the back seat, there are times when you can legally exceed the posted speed limit. "How is this possible?" you ask.

Some states have what are known as *prima facie* speed limits, while others have absolute speed limits. If you are cited for speeding in a state that has *prima facie* speed limits, you have the opportunity to try and prove that the speed you were traveling at was safe. This is really not that difficult. Any reasonable judge, after listening to you explain that the weather was clear, no one was on the road, and there were no school children around, will consider your speed accordingly and probably dismiss your case – despite the fact that you were going 45 m.p.h. in a 35 m.p.h. zone, when you were cited. Folks, this happens a lot more than you think. So rush down to your local library or DMV, get a copy of your state's vehicle code and find out if your state has *prima facie* speed limits.

Inaccurate Speedometer

Some people have been successful in getting speeding tickets dismissed by arguing that, unknown to them, their speedometer was off at the time of the violation.

If you suspect a faulty speedometer, and want to use this argument, you need to check it. You can do this by going to your local auto shop and having them test it. If it is off (in your favor), get some documentation that you can present to the judge. Another way to check your speedometer is with those five–mile speed checks located on many stretches of open freeway and highway. If you don't know what I am talking about or don't know of one near you, don't bother. Just go to the auto shop. Anyway, when you pass the "Mile 0" sign going 60 m.p.h. start your stop watch. Holding steady at 60 m.p.h., it should take you <u>exactly</u> five minutes to reach the "Mile 5–End Speed Check" sign. Don't forget to watch for cops. You will be "speeding." If it takes more than five minutes, your speedometer is off all right, but not in your favor. If it takes less than five minutes, then it is off in your favor. When you present this argument to the judge, documentation from an auto shop is much stronger evidence than just your testimony that "I checked the speedometer, your Honor, and it reads a higher speed than I am actually going."

Other Violations

It is my experience and belief that there is really one good way to beat a non–speeding ticket once you get to trial and the officer shows up. You must, however, do a little reading and a little thinking to be successful. Let me simplify this for you. When you received your citation, you allegedly violated a section of the vehicle code. Each section of the vehicle code has several parts to it, even though sometimes it may not always seem that way. The importance of this point is that in order for you to be found guilty of that section of the vehicle code for which you were cited, you must be guilty of each and every part within the section. Here is an example: This is section 22103 of the California Vehicle Code pertaining to prohibited u–turns:

> "No person in a residential district shall make a u-turn when any other vehicle is approaching from either direction within 200 feet except at an intersection when the approaching vehicle is controlled by an official traffic control device."

In order for you to be guilty of violating the section above, you must have been:

1. Operating a vehicle.

2. Driving in a residential district.

3. Making a u–turn.

4. Making your u–turn when a vehicle was ap–proaching either in front of or behind you.

5. Within 200 feet of the vehicle approaching.

The section goes on to say that your u–turn would be perfectly legal if the approaching vehicle was "controlled by an official traffic control device." Translated into English, this means traffic light, stop sign, etc. The officer has to prove beyond a reasonable doubt that you were guilty of <u>each</u> part of the section. If he doesn't, you walk. You see, our legal system does not allow you to be found partly guilty. It's all or nothing. The object here is to pick a certain part of the section you allegedly violated, preferably the one most wide open to interpretation, and try to prove that you were not guilty of that part. If you can accomplish this, the entire section is nullified because you must be guilty of all of it in order to be found guilty.

Please understand that "technically" you don't have to prove anything. The cop has the burden of proof. You are innocent until proven guilty. But in reality it doesn't always work this way. It definitely won't hurt your case to do a little proving of your own. Judges seem to be giving cops a lot of slack.

Sometimes it is not even necessary to prove that you were not guilty of the part in question. If you can raise any doubt, or the officer seems a little unsure of himself in any aspect of the case, then you may have raised enough doubt to get the charges dismissed.

Let's take the u–turn law as an example, tear it apart, and look at its guts. Obviously parts 1 and 3 can be ignored because you *were* operating a vehicle and you almost certainly made a u–turn. Part 2 could be open to question. Were you in a residential district? What is a residential district? You may say, "Well, that's easy. It's where there are lots of houses around." Maybe. I've seen lots of houses in districts that are zoned "business" by the city, so there could be an argument here. You would want to pay a quick visit to the city planning department in this case to check and see if the area where you were cited was zoned "residential." Part 4 could also be open to the question of whether there were any cars around you.

Part 5 brings distance into the picture. It says that no vehicle can be within 200 feet of you when you make your turn. Well, this seems simple, but exactly how far is 200 feet? Where was this cop when he claimed there was a vehicle within 200 feet of you? How could he tell the distance? I mean, you weren't driving down a football field with yard–line markers. Ask him how he measured that distance. If he stutters, stalls, or is unsure in any way, you probably have a good case against him. This might be a good time for another fun courtroom demonstration. Ask the officer to estimate the distance diagonally from one corner of the courtroom to the other. Bring a tape measure with you. The bailiff can use it to determine the actual distance after the officer has given his guess. Then make your attack on the officer's judgment accordingly.

It would be a good idea for you to return to the site of the violation and do some measurements yourself. When you get to court you'll already have the answers. If the cop comes up with some bogus number, politely tell the judge that you returned to the site, measured the distance, and that the officer must be mistaken.

So you see, this isn't as hard as it sounds, but, like I said, it does require doing a little bit of homework. The first and foremost step in this homework assignment is to get a copy of the vehicle code book, which can be obtained from your local library or the DMV. Find the section which you supposedly violated. Then take the section apart, like I just did with the u–turn section. If you have time, try to read the whole vehicle code book. You'll be surprised how much you'll learn.

Something else that may help your case is making an effort to shed some doubt on the officer's memory or judgment. The easiest way to do this is to *barrage the officer with a bunch of questions* that you already know the answers to, about the ticket and the circumstances surrounding the violation. *For example:*

1. *What color or kind of clothes was I wearing?*
2. *What was the weather like?*
3. *Did I have any passengers?*
4. *What did they look like?*
5. *Was there a full moon?*

This line of questioning can go on forever, but if the officer answers enough of the questions incorrectly, or doesn't answer, it starts to look like he really wasn't paying much attention to what was going on. So how, therefore, could he possibly be correct in his testimony regarding your violation? Be sure to keep the questions relevant though, or the judge will shut you up. Take the offensive. Attack the officer (not literally) and make him feel nervous. When you do, chances are he'll screw up somewhere. After all, he's not used to being attacked. Most people are afraid of him. At the same time make sure that you are polite and respectful. If you start getting cocky, angry or otherwise emotional, you might as well pay your fine and leave.

Red Lights

Many people think that if a light turns red while they are in an intersection, they're guilty of running a red light. Not true. Here's the rule: If any part of your vehicle enters the intersection before the light turns red, you're clear. The reasoning is simple. If your car is already in the intersection when the opposing traffic gets a green light, they're obviously not going to take off and plow into you. On the other hand, if you enter the intersection after your light has turned red, the opposing traffic will probably already be moving. An accident is likely, and you're a fool for pushing your luck.

If you get a citation for running a red light from a cop who was on the opposing side of the intersection, ask the following when you get to court. "Officer, how can you say my light was red if you couldn't see it?" He will invariably reply: "Because my light was green." Then ask: "Do you know for sure that the instant my light turned red yours turned green?" "Did you check the coordination of the lights both before and after you cited me?" The answer to the last question is almost always no, and therefore a doubt has been raised. Check the coordination of the lights yourself. If they're off, even by a fraction of a second, your case just got much better.

Unmarked Cars

I once received a ticket from a cop who, when he pulled me over, was driving a two–tone red and gray Ford Taurus station wagon. I thought to myself, is this a joke or what? These guys must be really desperate. This wagon was totally unmarked, no stickers, no insignia, no official looking paint job, no nothing. Since then I have seen and heard about unmarked cars in all sorts of shapes, sizes and colors. The reason I am sharing this with you is so that you can be aware, if you're not already, of the fact that cops prowl around in unmarked cars quite often. Depending on what state you live in, there is usually some kind of law prohibiting officers from issuing citations while operating unmarked cars. But these laws usually have built in escape clauses and loopholes that allow the officers to get away with it in "special circumstances."

There are a couple of things you should keep in mind if you ever find yourself being pulled over by an unmarked "squad car." First, there are people out there who run around impersonating police officers and robbing people. With that in mind, if you are going to pull over, wait until you get to a populated area or a well lit place before stopping. On the other hand, you might just keep on going and not pull over at all. If it is a real cop, he will probably call for backup and you will cause a big scene which will actually probably work out in your favor since cops don't like big scenes surrounding "unmarked" cars. If it's not a real cop you will have avoided being robbed. Anyway, this is just a suggestion. The decision is up to you.

7

LAWYERS

Do You Need One?

Before you begin your actual pilgrimage to the courthouse you may want to consider consulting a lawyer. If you are a person who is fortunate enough to have excessive amounts of cash lying around, then go see a lawyer. He or she can give you specific insight into your case and help you out quite a bit. If there is a technical or legal angle of your case that has a good chance for dismissal but needs some knowledge of legal procedure, a lawyer can be very useful and adept at handling this for you. A lawyer will also be very good at plea bargaining with the prosecution for you if you have a serious offense like reckless driving. Be selective when choosing a lawyer for your case. Many lawyers consider traffic cases trivial and are therefore not very knowledgeable about them.

Most of us don't fall into the "got bucks" category and most lawyers are very expensive. So, although lawyers can be helpful, they often cost more than their advice is worth for a small thing like a traffic violation. There is, however, an exception to this: drunk driving. Until now I have said almost nothing about this. It is usually a good idea to get a lawyer when the situation involves drinking and driving. Chapter 9 is dedicated completely to drunk driving violations.

As far as locating a good attorney for your case, here's a method that seems to work very well, not only for drunk driving, but for anything else for which you might need legal consultation or assistance. Go through your local phone book and call every single attorney and law office in there. Ask them who are the three attorneys that they would most highly recommend, besides themselves. When you are all finished you should have one or two frequently recommended names and they are probably your best bet. Remember, a recommendation from a colleague and/or a competitor is a strong one.

By the way, the National Motorists Association [(608) 849–6000] has a legal referral service to help people looking for a good traffic lawyer. You may want to give them a call also. If you should decide to join the NMA, you should know about a very special deal they offer for people who have been members for at least one year. If a renewing member gets a speeding ticket, goes to court and fights it, but still loses, THEY WILL PAY FOR THE TICKET. They do this because they, like the author, want you to fight your ticket! For obvious reasons it is highly recommended that you join this organization.

8

TRAFFIC COURT AND ARRAIGNMENT

They're Not As Intimidating As You Think

Arraignment

Up until now we haven't discussed any specifics on how traffic court and trials work, so here they are. On the bottom of your citation is the location of a municipal or justice court and a date. You must show up at that court on or before that date and do one of two things. If you are pleading not guilty, you can go straight to the clerk, plead not guilty in writing and ask for a trial. Or you may choose to attend what is known as arraignment. Several things can happen at arraignment. You are asked to enter a plea – guilty, no contest or not guilty. If you plead guilty, the judge assesses a fine, you pay it, and you are on your way, finished, end of story. Your ticket goes to the DMV as a conviction and your insurance company usually begins reaming you shortly thereafter.

If you plead no contest, the exact same thing happens. The only time you will want to use a "no contest" plea is when your ticket was issued as a result of your involvement in an accident. A "no contest" plea will prevent whoever you were in the accident with from using your plea as evidence in a civil suit against you later. If you plead not guilty, then a trial date is set for you to return. You will be asked to pay the bail amount of the ticket at this point. If you win they send you a check; if you lose they keep the money. You may be asked whether you want an informal or formal trial. However they define the difference, just make sure that the type of trial you get is one with the officer present as the prosecutor or state's witness. You have a legal right to this. After all, one of your main objectives is to get the officer not to show up so your case will be dismissed. If you have time, it would be a great idea to sit

in at an arraignment hearing before you have to go to yours. It will make you feel a lot more at ease to know a little about the judge and his procedures before you take the stand.

Twenty–four states in this country allow you to request a jury trial for a traffic violation. If you exercise this option, here's what to expect. First, a bunch of irritated people. All the way from the judge to the jurors. Jury trials cost the court system, thus taxpayers, a lot of time and money. You won't be popular for requesting a jury trial. The jurors are already being inconvenienced. When they find out they had to take off work to decide on your speeding ticket they'll probably be even less happy. Almost all traffic violations are handled in traffic court and they'll wonder what makes you think you're so special.

In addition, you'll probably have a prosecutor assigned to your case instead of just a police officer. It is likely that he has a lot more courtroom expertise than a cop. He may decide to make an example out of you, unless you have an attorney to stand up for you. This is not meant to discourage you from requesting a jury trial. It is meant to give you an idea of what you may be up against. If you pursue the jury trial alternative, a competent lawyer is recommended.

In case you were wondering, drunk driving is different. At present only two states, California and New Jersey, do not allow jury trials for DUI (Driving Under the Influence), or DWI (Driving While Intoxicated), offenses. Nevada only allows them on felony drunk driving cases. Felony drunk driving means you were involved in an accident and someone was hurt or killed as a result.

Pre–Trial Motions

At the arraignment, you may use a couple of different requests that are known as pretrial motions. You may request that you do not want a certain judge at your trial because you feel that he or she is prejudiced in some way towards you or your violation. You can also do this when you get to trial. In most cases, traffic court judges are on rotation so you usually won't know which one you'll get until you arrive. Also, if you requested your citing officer to designate the trial at the county seat and he refused, you may request this again at arraignment and your request will most likely be granted at this point.

Traffic School

In some jurisdictions – and it varies from county to county and state to state – at the arraignment you may request to attend traffic school in exchange for having your ticket dismissed. If it is available and you can afford the extra expense, I highly recommend taking advantage of this opportunity. It will keep your ticket off your driving record and your insurance rates from going up as a result. As stated earlier, they cost way more in the long run than the ticket. Traffic school usually costs somewhere around $35 (rates do vary so check around) and is most commonly held on weekends but is also offered on weekdays and evenings in many cases. Traffic school is usually a breeze, especially if you live in California where they have schools with names like; "Wheel Make You Laugh," "Lettuce Amuse You," "Laugh's Galore–U Won't Snore" and, last but not least, "Comedy For Less, No Work No Test!" If you don't, not to worry. Wherever you live, traffic school is not something you flunk. Traffic schools are in business to make money and educate people, but not to flunk them.

When you finish you get a completion certificate. It is either sent, or you have to send it, to the court where your case was heard. The ticket is then dismissed. You are limited in most jurisdictions to only one traffic school attendance per year, although some allow more and some allow less. Also, in some states, you must pay the bail amount on the ticket in order to attend traffic school. It used to be that you only had to pay traffic school costs, but these days the bureaucrats need more money. If however, you feel you have a really good case and chance of winning, skip traffic school and go to court. When you win, you don't pay.

Traffic Court

So you went to arraignment, pleaded not guilty and requested a trial. The trial date they gave you was probably about a month away. The month goes by and you head for the courthouse. When you get there you will probably need to check in with the clerk. If you have any witnesses who will testify in your favor, bring them. The best witnesses are usually passengers. Just make sure you have all your facts straight. It's not a good sign when you and your witnesses contradict each other. Be on time. If you are too late they may lock you out. Even if they don't, you'll start off on the wrong foot with the judge. The judge will usually "take roll" before proceedings begin to see who showed up and who didn't. This is so the cops whose defendants didn't show up can get on with their day and defendants whose cops didn't show up can do likewise. If your luck is good, your cop won't show, your case will be dismissed and you won't be there but maybe 10 minutes. If your luck isn't good, he will show and you will sit and wait until your case is called. Two things to remember when you are waiting to be called. First, be calm, collected and very polite at all times. Address the judge as "your Honor" and the cop as "Officer." Second, the cop has the burden of proof. You are innocent until proven guilty beyond a reasonable doubt. He has to establish that you are guilty. You only need to raise a reasonable doubt that you are not.

When your case is called you (and your witnesses, if you have any) and the officer will go up to the front of the room. Both sides get to tell their story to the judge. The officer goes first and basically tells the judge when, where, why, how and what he observed you doing and what you were cited for. TAKE NOTES. Pay attention to what he says, so you can capitalize on his mistakes. You vividly recall what happened. It was a traumatic experience for you. He won't, unless you really did something out of the ordinary. He writes tickets every day and the only way he remembers the details is from his notes. If he didn't take good notes (often they don't) he's a fish out of water. If you feel like he might be ad libbing his testimony, you can request to see his notes. You can also ask him to explain what they mean. If you find him giving testimony that's not on the ticket or anywhere in his notes, point this out to the judge later. Explain that you find it hard to believe that the officer could be sure about anything that happened that long and that many tickets ago unless it was written down.

As the officer is giving his opening testimony he may begin testifying with inadmissible evidence to back him up. Here's an example. The officer states that he clocked you at a certain speed with his radar unit.

Before a police officer can use the radar reading as evidence, he needs to establish the following:

1. He had jurisdiction to use radar on the roadway where he cited you.

2. He has a certified, up to date, accurate, traffic and engineering survey, if applicable.

3. His radar unit was properly calibrated.

4. His tuning forks were properly calibrated.

5. His agency has a license with the FCC to use radar.

6. His radar unit appears on that FCC license.

If he hasn't established any or all of these, the radar reading may be inadmissible evidence. If so, he can't use it against you. You would politely interrupt the officer and address the judge by saying, "Objection, your Honor, inadmissible evidence," if the officer began to testify in such a manner. The reason that the evidence is inadmissible is because the officer has not established justification for using it.

Another type of testimony that you may wish to object to is known as "hearsay." The rule is: An officer cannot testify to anything that is outside of his own personal knowledge or experience. Here's an example: You received a ticket from a cop who was assisted by an air patrolman. If the cop begins to talk about how the officer in the plane clocked you, then this is hearsay. He wasn't there, he didn't do it himself and therefore cannot testify about it.

When the officer finishes his opening testimony, quickly evaluate what he said. If he did not establish that you violated each and every element of the section he cited you for, ask the judge to dismiss your case.

Here's an example. Let's say you were cited for violating the code pertaining to u–turns discussed in Chapter 6. Remember that in order to be guilty of that violation it must be established that you were:

1. Operating a vehicle.
2. Driving in a residential district.
3. Making a u–turn.
4. Making your u–turn when a vehicle was approaching either in front of or behind you.
5. Within 200 feet of the vehicle approaching.

It is a good idea to take this type of list to court with you. As the officer testifies, check off the elements he establishes you violated. Let's say that the officer failed to mention in his testimony that there was a vehicle approaching you less than 200 feet away. In so doing he failed to establish that you are guilty. Remember, you're innocent until the officer has proven that you are guilty.

When the officer finished his testimony you would request the judge to dismiss your case: "Your Honor, I move to have this case dismissed. The officer did not introduce any evidence that established that there was a vehicle approaching me from less than 200 feet away." This approach works sometimes. Usually the judge will give the cop a second chance and let him fill in what he left out.

©Franz Krachtus'92

If your case is not dismissed you move on to the cross–examination. This means you get to ask the officer questions. This is your opportunity to grill him. You should have your list ready, as well as several different angles of attack depending on how he answers your questions. If you are going to use any of the "courtroom demonstrations" that attack the officer's speed or distance estimation abilities described in earlier chapters, now is the time. They are highly recommended. Ask him trick questions and try to get him in a corner, where he says; "I do not recall" or contradicts himself about what really happened.

Now you get to establish your defense. It is at this point that you present all of your evidence. Remember that everything you testify to must be from your personal knowledge also. If somebody else did it or said it, don't waste your breath. Clear pictures and diagrams are great at this point as long as they directly illustrate some aspect of why you are not guilty. When presenting these, don't assume that the judge knows the area in question. Pretend he's never been there before. Design and describe everything clearly.

Throughout this book countless defenses, weaknesses and arguments have been outlined for you. Pick out those that might apply to your particular case. Write them down and put them in logical order. Rehearse them; practice your argument. Take notes to court with you and have them right in front of you. Be ready to shift gears in midstream and change your attack depending on how your questions are answered. Make this a fun challenge. Be confident and sure of yourself. Believe that you are going to win. If it's a speeding violation, you would present all of your evidence about VASCAR, radar or visual estimation, and how under the circumstances they must have been inaccurate. If you requested radar certification documents or a traffic engineering survey that were not provided, or received some that were inaccurate or out of date, you would capitalize on these facts. If you have proof that your speedometer was inaccurate, present that. If the lady in your car was pregnant or you were cited on a *prima facie* road and believe your speed was safe, say so. If the officer did not use a tuning fork to calibrate his unit, throw that at the judge too. If the officer answered any of your questions incorrectly, didn't answer them or contradicted himself, present this in your evidence also.

Your witnesses are part of your defense too. If you have any, now is the time to present them. You can, and may, prompt your witness(es) by asking them specific questions to get the testimony you want out of them. This can save you from witness(es) contradicting your testimony.

When you finish, rest your case but let the judge know you would like to make a final statement. The officer goes first but will usually have little, if anything to say. Then you lay it on thick and heavy.

In closing, rather than accuse the officer of being "wrong," say that the officer must have been mistaken. You might state that you are an honest, law abiding citizen and that you honestly believe you are innocent of the violation in question. Be earnest and sincere. The judge will feel that. Before you enter the courtroom, believe that you really are innocent, and that you are just an unfortunate victim of the system. When you are convinced that you are innocent, you are on a crusade, you have a moral conviction. Then it becomes a whole different ball game.

If at all possible, I highly recommend that you pick a day before your actual court date and go down to the courthouse and sit in on a day of traffic proceedings. It will be a tremendous help to you. You'll get to know the judge, what he likes, what he doesn't, how his courtroom functions and basically what you are in for.

For those of you who would rather write than speak your mind, there is an alternative to this whole court trial business. It's called "trial by declaration." It amounts to being a mail in trial. You write out your case and arguments and send them to the judge. He decides, then mails you his decision. You can request this option from the clerk or at arraignment. This is not recommended, because you miss out on two very important things: the possibility of the officer not showing, and the opportunity to cross–examine him if he does.

Finally, even if you lose, you still have the option to appeal your case to a higher court. If you do, there are a couple of things to consider. You are then getting into spending even more money and time (appealing isn't free). On the other hand, very few people ever take traffic cases to Superior Court. If and when you do, you <u>will</u> get the judge's attention. He will probably guess that you must think you have a good case; otherwise you wouldn't have come this far (or he may just think you're a nut). But if you have a good, solid case, your chances of winning in Superior Court are usually much better than they are in traffic court.

©Franz Krachtus 92

HAVE YOU BEEN
DRINKING TODAY?

9

DRUNK DRIVING

Before And After The Field Sobriety Test

Before beginning this chapter, I would like to state that I am very much opposed to drunk driving. I lost three close friends to a drunk driver a few years back, and the irresponsibility of that individual is not easily forgiven. However, I am not a neoprohibitionist and I feel that there is a difference between driving "drunk" and having a glass of wine with dinner and then driving home. In line with that thought, here's a quote for you to think about. It comes from a lady by the name of Candace Lightner, who founded MADD (Mothers Against Drunk Drivers):

> *"Lowering the legal blood–alcohol level from .10 percent to .08 percent will not affect the real cause of the majority of crashes: Drivers with BAC (Blood Alcohol Content) levels well above .10... Legislation and enforcement should concentrate on the problem drinkers rather than shifting the focus to include social drinkers with lower BAC's."*

That, as they say, comes straight from the horse's mouth. It came from an article that she wrote in opposition to pending legislation lowering the legal BAC in Virginia to .08 percent. Like Candace, the author does not condone drunk driving. But with the advent of things such as roadblocks and zero–tolerance laws, enforcement is expanding beyond the scope of the real problem.

Let's begin with a couple of words about when you are first pulled over and you've been drinking. When the officer pulls you over he will approach your door and shine that blinding flashlight right in your face, look you straight in the eyes, and watch what

Franz Krachtus '92

your pupils do. Your pupils are those little dark spots in the middle of your eyes that open and close depending on how light it is. If you are drunk, or alcohol impaired in any way, your pupils will react more slowly to light than if you were sober. When the officer watches your pupils close very slowly, while his flashlight beams in your face, it gives him a good indication that you are under the influence of something. If you can do so without it appearing to the officer that you might be reaching for a weapon, try to get your license and registration out. Hopefully, you are organized enough so that by the time the officer gets to you, you have everything ready to hand to him. After the officer completes his initial interrogation, he will decide whether to let you go or carry his evaluation further. If he says, "Step out of the car, please," that's when your real troubles begin.

Another thing to think about is the fact that your car could be towed. If you've been drinking there is a good chance that you are going to spend the night in jail. Your car, of course, is going to spend the night wherever you pull over. So try for a legal parking spot; otherwise, after you get out of jail, you may have to go bail your car out of the local towing yard.

When and if the officer asks that inevitable question, "How much have you had to drink tonight?" your best response to that accusing inquiry depends on the situation. Just remember that anything you say can be used against you in court. If you feel that you are obviously drunk, lying to the officer about how much you have or have not had to drink won't do you any good because he is still going to give you the roadside sobriety test. Furthermore, lying to an officer won't help you at all if you go to court later. Usually if you admit to drinking anything you are guaranteed subjection to the sobriety test. The reason for this is that most people admit to drinking much less than they really drank and cops know this.

So you've never been lucky enough to experience the road-side sobriety test? Well, here's a little about it to prepare you just in case you find yourself in that unfortunate situation some day. First, legally, you do not have to submit to any of these coordination tests. If you do decide to refuse you will accomplish two things. Number one, you will make the hair on the back of the officer's neck stand up. He will not be happy. Number two, you will give him a lot less evidence for testifying against you later in court.

Anyway, *the officer will ask you to perform a series of simple coordination tests after he asks you to step out of the car. These tests may include any or all of the following:*

1. *Touching your fingers together or to your nose with your eyes closed.*
2. *Walking in a straight line.*
3. *Counting from 1–10 and back down again.*
4. *Repeating the alphabet.*
5. *Standing on one leg.*

It is not a bad idea to practice these "exercises." Many people can't perform them adequately when they are stone cold sober. These tests are deliberately designed to give a cop probable cause for a blood alcohol content (BAC) test. Lack of probable cause is one of the few defenses against a DUI (Driving Under the Influence) or DWI (Driving While Intoxicated) conviction.

From these tests, your eyes and your speech, an officer will determine whether he has cause to subject you to one of the three BAC tests. If you refuse to take one of these tests, the DMV will usually automatically suspend your license regardless of whether you are found not guilty of drunk driving later. So, unfortunately, it is almost always in your best interest to submit to one of the tests.

The three tests you have to choose from are the breath test, the urine test and the blood test.

These tests are designed to determine the actual alcohol content in your body. The blood test almost always gives the most accurate blood alcohol level reading of the three tests. It is much harder to cast doubt on the results of this particular test later in court.

© Franz Krachtus '92

WHAT WOULD YOU LIKE ?
URINE SAMPLE, BLOOD SAMPLE...

The breath test is also pretty accurate, but you may want to consider taking it if you've had very little to drink. The reason for this is that the breath test produces immediate results. If they are low enough the officer will probably let you go right then, but then again he may not. You see, if an officer pulls you over for drunk driving, lets you go and you proceed to get in an accident and kill someone, his career is probably finished and he is subject to a serious lawsuit. So don't be surprised if he doesn't let you go. Here is another note about taking the breath test, or breathalyzer as it is commonly called. When you submit to this test, the officer will try to get the longest, deepest possible breath out of you. The reason for this is simple. The longer the air stays in your lungs, the more saturated with alcohol it becomes, and thus the higher the reading.

Your third choice is the urine test. Of the three tests this is usually the most inaccurate and, therefore, most open to question. It can give misleadingly high or low readings depending on how long it's been since you consumed your last drink or urinated. This can work to your advantage or disadvantage. Regardless, it is much easier for an experienced attorney to dispute the results of a urine test than the results of the others. Another available option with the urine test is that you can request your own sample. You can then take this sample to an independent lab and get a "second opinion" on your blood alcohol level. If there's a discrepancy between the test results, it can be the basis for a dismissal. This option also applies to the blood test but obviously not the "breathalyzer."

So, you've taken one of the tests and you flunked. You are now the lucky recipient of an overnight ticket to the drunk tank. To make things worse, you are being charged with driving under the influence. So what's next? Well, after you get out of jail it is my advice that you follow only one route: get a lawyer. If you can't afford one, be sure to ask the judge to appoint one at your first court appearance. Drunk driving carries with it some rather hefty penalties. Unless you really know your way around a courtroom, you should not try to defend yourself.

Be aware that a drunk driving charge carries with it the

possibility of two separate violations. You can obviously be convicted of driving under the influence, but you can also be convicted of driving with a blood alcohol level of .08 or over. Believe it or not, these are two separate charges and violations. Your blood alcohol level is determined when you take one of the three tests discussed earlier. If the results show that the level of alcohol in your blood was .08, or higher, you will automatically be convicted of driving with a blood alcohol level of .08 or more – even if you can prove that you were not driving under the influence. At present a large number of states still have .10 legal BAC levels, but legislators nationwide are pressing hard to get all the legal BAC levels down to .08 – some even lower. Find out the limit in your state and then keep track of it!

Driving under the influence is a completely relative concept. While a few people can be under the influence and impaired with a blood alcohol level of .06, others do not even feel the effects of alcohol until their blood alcohol level is in excess of .10. Our states have just arbitrarily decided that at a .08 or .10 blood alcohol level, you are "legally" drunk. Whether or not you were actually under the influence (alcohol impaired) is basically up to the officer. If he testifies that you were weaving all over the road and flunked the roadside test, there is not too much you can do to dispute him regardless of what your blood alcohol level was. Therefore, it is possible for you to be convicted of either one or both of the charges depending on the situation and circumstances.

Now the bad news. Let's give you an idea of some of the penalties and consequences of DUI convictions. Showcased below, are California's generous gifts to drunk drivers. Some states are more generous and some a bit less, but you'll get the idea.

If you are pulled over and held on suspicion of drunk driving, your license will be taken from you on the spot. In exchange, you will receive a 45–day temporary driving permit. If you are asked to take the breath, blood or urine test, and fail or refuse to take one, your license will automatically be suspended for four months and that's only if you are a first offender. If you have one or more DUI convictions, your license will be suspended for at least one year.

Once your license is taken, you have ten days to appeal to the DMV, but you had better have a good case or excuse because they are not showing much mercy on drunk drivers. Unfortunately for you, there is a lot more at stake than just your driver's license in a DUI charge. The minimum penalties for a first DUI offense are: Four days in jail and attendance at an alcohol abuse class. If you get a really nice judge, he may only send you to jail for two days with the alcohol abuse class. This is in addition to your license suspension and whatever your insurance company decides to do with your rates. The maximum penalties for a first offense are a different story: Six months in the county jail, a $1,000 fine, and your car impounded for a month at your expense. The penalties get a lot more severe for repeat convictions. For example, a third DUI brings with it maximum penalties of at least a $1,000 fine, one year in jail, an automatic three–year license suspension and a three--month car impounding. You can also count on your insurance company dropping you like a hot potato. Then good luck getting auto insurance after that for less than $4,000 a year, if you can get it at all. Let's face it, repeated DUIs can really screw up your life.

California has also adopted, along with some other states, what they call a "zero tolerance law." In a nutshell it says that any drivers under the age of 21 will lose their license for a year and be fined $100 if they have ANY alcohol in their blood at all when tested. The unfortunate thing about this law is that it doesn't take into consideration the fact that some mouthwashes and nighttime cold medicines can give low blood alcohol readings. Who said anything about being fair?

Some states are now giving judges the discretion to sentence anyone convicted of a third DUI to obtain and maintain an "ignition interlock" device in their vehicle. This device measures their blood alcohol level and is connected to the ignition. If they register higher than the legal BAC level, their car will not start. Isn't it amazing what they can do with technology these days?

So how do you get out of a drunk driving charge? Well, it depends on how drunk you were. If your case was borderline, and you get a good attorney, he may be able to cast enough doubt on the test results and/or the officer's testimony to get the case dismissed. There is also a chance in a borderline or doubtful case that the prosecutor will consent to plea bargaining. In other words, you plead guilty to a lesser charge in exchange for the drunk driving charges being dropped. In most drunk driving cases that lesser charge is reckless driving. Other than that, once again I must say your only hope is to get your hands on the best attorney you can find and talk your options over with him or her.

10

INSURANCE

Do You Have To Have It? How Do You Get It?

In at least 40 of our states, the law says you have to have some kind of auto insurance. In some states when an officer pulls you over for any violation, he will ask you for three things, one of which is proof of insurance. If you don't have insurance, or left your little proof of insurance card that your insurance company gives you, at home, then you get a citation for not having proof of insurance in addition to whatever the officer pulled you over for in the first place. You then need to show proof of insurance at arraignment in order to get that charge dismissed. So if you don't have insurance, don't get in an accident. Better yet, don't drive. If you do, you could put yourself in debt for life. This is especially true when you consider the way people are suing each other these days.

Buying insurance can be a complicated undertaking. Start in the phone book and follow the same procedure recommended earlier to find an attorney. Prices, coverage, and companies vary greatly, so shopping around is essential. Depending on the condition of your driving record, you may be very limited in what you have to choose from. Many companies will not insure anyone with a lot of tickets. The ones that do can be astronomically expensive. However, beware of those insurance "companies" advertising that they can insure anyone, no matter what their driving record. Rumors abound that some of these companies charge outrageous rates. Then, if you ever have a claim, they manage one way or another through legal jargon or disclaimers to disqualify your claim. You are then left to pick up the tab. If you are really interested in protecting yourself, your vehicle, and anyone you might injure, you should make an effort to find at least a somewhat reputable company. Otherwise, if you are involved in an accident, you may find yourself in deep snow.

© Franz Krachtus '92

WELL, BECAUSE YOU'RE IN THE
"HIGH RISK BRACKET" THE
BEST WE CAN DO IS $ 6,342
PER YEAR.

11

THE END

What You Need To Do

In conclusion, keep these three things in mind:

1. Always pay attention.
2. Keep your eyes open for cops.
3. Always fight your ticket whenever you possibly can.

You owe it to yourself, your country and mankind as a whole. If everyone went to court and fought their tickets, cops would spend most of their time in courtrooms and the court system would be overflowing with ticket cases. If that happened, a lot of laws would change and cops would no longer be expected to waste their time issuing trivial tickets. They would only write tickets when there was a flagrant violation involved. But, as the system works now, it is a big money–making rip–off scam, because most people pay the astronomical "bail" amounts and then in turn pay even more money to their insurance company.

By the way, a friend gave me a copy of the radar trainee instruction manual, which is given to officers when they are first being trained to use radar. It is put out by the U.S. Department of Transportation and the National Highway Traffic Safety Administration. Here's a paragraph in it that you may find quite amusing:

> "It is hoped that every officer who
> completes this course will become a
> better enforcer of the traffic laws
> governing vehicle speed – that is, the
> officer will detect more speed viola-
> tions, apprehend more violators, and
> secure more convictions."

Don't you think what they meant to say was, "make more money?" The author would like to offer a few words to the many law enforcement officers who pick up this book out of curiosity or give copies of it to their colleagues as gag gifts, specifically those of you whom we motorists generally refer to as "gung ho cops." Remember that we are humans just like you, and we are motorists just like you. When you are writing one of us a ticket, put yourself in our shoes and ask yourself: Does this person really deserve this ticket and all of the pain, anguish and financial hardship that goes along with it? Is there any real reason to treat this person as a criminal?

We have all heard your excuse: "Hey, I'm just doing my job." But what is your job, really? Isn't your job to serve and protect us? You know as well as we do that you have, for all intents and purposes, become a tax collector. Why do most of you deny it? Are you embarrassed? Are you afraid? Take a step back and think about what you are doing. When you get into your patrol car and head off to work tomorrow, make an effort to think about protect-ing and helping us instead of trapping and persecuting us.

As kids, most of us were taught to respect a police officer, but in this day and age, many among us, especially the younger generation, despise law enforcement officers and have little or no respect for them. This is not right and it's too bad. You, the police officer, do not deserve the brunt of all the anger and resentment that people feel toward you. After all, you are basically doing what you are told. The people who deserve to catch most of the flak are a long way above you in the government hierarchy, but the average citizen does not see them as the antagonist. They see you. So you find yourself in an interesting situation. Although you yourself aren't the cause of the problem, you can most definitely be the solution! You have the power, the ability and the authority to change the way we feel about you and treat you. All you have to do is treat us like human beings instead of "prey." You might be surprised at how quickly we will begin to respect you again for the police officer you are instead of fearing you for the loaded gun you carry at your side, and hating you for the ticket book you carry in your hand.

Anyway, that being said, the rest of you, for everybody's sake, GO FIGHT YOUR TICKET! And good luck. If you have any comments or suggestions about anything in this book, please write me, because I am anxious to hear if my experiences have helped you. This is an ongoing crusade and you can be part of it. If you have any stories, information, or clippings you would like to contribute, please send them in. They are greatly appreciated.

©Franz Krachteus '92

IS THAT A TICKET BOOK
IN YOUR POCKET OR ARE
YOU JUST HAPPY TO SEE ME?

Resources

Other Books With Similar Subject Material:

1. Fight Your Ticket
David Brown, Nolo Press, Ph. (415) 549-1976

2. How To Win In Traffic Court
Phil Bello, Major Market Books. 146 S. Lakeview Dr Ste. 300, Gibbsboro, NJ 08026

3. Traffic Court: How To Win
James Glass, Allenby Press. 701 First Ave Ste. 272, Arcadia, CA 91006

4. A Former Prosecutor Tells How To Win Your Case In Traffic Court
Charles Rubin, 1888 Century Park East, L. A., CA 90067, Ph. (213) 879-0111

5. The Ticket Book
Rod Dornsife, P.O. Box 1087. La Jolla, CA 92038

6. A Speeder's Guide To Avoiding Tickets
James Eagan, Avon Books

7. Beating The Radar Rap
John Tomerlin, Ph. 1-800-448-5170

8. How To Talk Your Way Out Of A Traffic Ticket
David Kelley, Mark III Productions, P. O. Box 586, Yuba City,

CA 95992

9. 101+ Ways To Get Out Of A Traffic Ticket
Jeff Hodge, Talent World Productions, P. O. Box 711090. Houston, TX 77271

10. Your Driving And The Law
Carol Haas

Law Enforcement Publications Of Interest:

1. Air Beat Magazine .... a magazine for airpatrolmen, 3740 Kimberly Way, Carmichael, CA 95608, Ph. (916) 922-6547

2. The Journal .... official publication of the National Fraternal Order Of Police, 2100 Gardiner #103A, Louisville, KY 40205, Ph. (502) 451-2700

3. Law Enforcement Technology .... technical magazine for police, 445 Broad Hollow Rd., Ste. 21, Melville, NY 11747, Ph. (516) 845-2700

4. Law and Order .... general magazine for police, 1000 Skokie Blvd., Wilmette, IL 60091, Ph. (708) 256-8555

5. National Bulletin on Police Misconduct
131 Beverly, Boston, MA 02114, Ph. (617) 542-0048

6. Police Times Magazine .... publication of American Federation of Police, 3801 Biscayne Blvd., Miami, FL 33137, Ph. (305) 573-0070

Auto and Traffic Association Publications of Interest:

1. NMA News.. publication of the National Motorists Association, 6678 Pertzborn Rd Dane. WI 53529, Ph. (608) 849-6000

2. NMA Motorist's Guide to State and Provincial Traffic Laws .... publication of the National Motorists Association, 6678 Pertzborn Rd Dane. WI 53529, Ph. (608) 849-6000

3. AAMVA Bulletin .... publication of the American Association of Motor Vehicle Administrators, Ph. (202) 296-1955, 1201 Connecticut Ave. N.W. Ste. 910, Washington D.C. 20036

4. The AASHTO Journal .... publication of the American Association of State Highway and Transportation Officials, 444 N. Capitol St., Ste. 225, Washington D.C. 20001, Ph. (202) 624-5800

5. From The State Capitols .... Motor   Vehicle Regulation, P.O. Box 1939, New Haven, CT 06509 Ph. (203) 562-8518

6. AAA World Magazine .... publication of the American Automobile Association, 1000 AAA Dr. Heathrow, FL 32746, Ph. (407) 444-8544

7. RADAR .... publication on drivers rights, radar and other issues, 4949 S. 25A, Tipp City, OH 45371, Ph. (513) 667-5472

8. Ticket Fighters Paralegal Service.......... 2036 Columbus Parkway, #116, Benicia, CA 94510, Ph. (510) 524-7490

Magazines of Interest

1. AutoWeek
1400 Woodbridge Ave., Detroit, MI 48207, Ph. (313) 446-6000

2. Automobile Magazine
717 Fifth Ave., New York, NY 10022, Ph. (212) 745-2100

3. Car & Driver
1633 Broadway, 42nd Fl. New York, NY 10019, Ph. (212) 767-6095

4. MotorTrend
8490 Sunset Blvd., Los Angeles, CA 90069, Ph. (310) 854-2222

5. Motor World
951 S. Oxford, #109, Los Angeles, CA 90006, Ph. (213) 732-3477

6. Road & Track
1633 Broadway, 42nd Fl., New York, NY 10019, Ph. (212) 767-6677

More Specialized Magazines of Interest

This list is for those of you who read this book and are auto enthusiasts of some sort. This is a very short list. There are well over two hundred magazines and newsletters that cater to everything from Sunbeam owners to Woodies. There's even a newsletter called Fins, Chrome and Steel, published by the Foreign Car Hater's Club of America.

If you would like to get the entire list, simply contact us and ask for it, it's free. We however, ask that you pay for postage and handling in the amount of $2.50.

1. 4-Wheel .... Ph. (310) 854-2718

2. 4WD Sport Utility .... Ph. (714) 635-9040

3. American Rodder .... Ph. (818) 889-4726

4. Automotive News .... Ph. (313) 446-6000

5. Business Driver .... Ph. (213) 376-8788

6. Car Craft .... Ph. (310) 854-2222

7. Car And Parts Magazine .... Ph. (513) 498-0803

8. Chrysler Power .... Ph. (818) 303-6220

9. Circle Track .... Ph. (310) 854-2222

10. Corvette Fever .... Ph. (313) 575-9400

11. Dune Buggies & Hot VWs .... Ph. (714) 979-2560

12. European Car .... Ph. (2l3) 820-3601

13. Fabulous Mustangs & Exotic Fords.... Ph. (213) 820-3601

14. Four Wheeler .... Ph. (212) 496-6100

15. Guide To Muscle Cars .... Ph. (213) 820-3601

16. Hemmings Motor News .... Ph. (802) 442-3101

17. Hi-Performance Mopar .... Ph. (201) 712-9300

18. Hot Rod .... Ph. (310) 854-2222

19. Hot Rod Show World .... Ph. (313) 373-2500

20. Kit Car .... Ph. (310) 854-2222

21. Mini Truckin' .... Ph. (613) 236-3535

22. Mopar Muscle Magazine .... Ph. (813) 644-0449

23. Motor Trend's Sports Cars
    of the World .... Ph. (310) 854-2222

24. Muscle Car Classics .... Ph. (310) 854-2222

25. Muscle Car Review .... Ph. (813) 644-0449

26. Muscle Cars of the 60's-70's .... Ph. (513) 498-0803

27. MuscleCars .... Ph. (201) 712-9300

28. Mustang .... Ph. (310) 854-2222

29. Mustang and Fords .... Ph. (310) 854-2222

30. Mustang Monthly .... Ph. (813) 646-5743

31. National Dragster .... Ph. (818) 963-7695

32. Off Road .... Ph. (213) 820-3601

33. Old Cars Weekly .... Ph. (715) 445-2214

34. Open Wheel Magazine .... Ph. (508) 356-7030

35. Performance for the Chrysler
    Car Enthusiast .... Ph. (215) 639-4456

36. Speedway Scene .... Ph. (508) 238-7016

37. Sport Truck .... Ph. (310) 854-2222

38. Sports Car .... Ph. (714) 259-8240

39. Sports Car International .... Ph. (714) 851-3924

40. Street Rodder .... Ph. (714) 778-3149

41. Super Chevy .... Ph. (213) 820-3601

42. Super Ford .... Ph. (813) 646-5743

43. Turbo & Hi-Tech Performance .... Ph. (714) 962-7795

44. VW Trends .... Ph. (714) 635-9040

45. Vette .... Ph. (201) 712-9300

46. World of Wheels .... Ph. (416) 297-9277

Note: If you are on this resource list and we for some reason have inaccurate information in your listing, please let us know.

Also if you would like to make sure that we have you correctly listed on our master list of over 200 publications, please drop us a line.

Thank you.

GLOSSARY

85th Percentile Rule–Rule stating that the speed 85% of drivers travel at or below, under normal conditions, on a given road, should be the posted speed limit on that road.

Absolute Speed Limits–Posted speed limits that may not be legally exceeded.

Accident Rate–Statistic used to compare the amount of accidents to the number of miles driven.

Air Patrolling–Speed enforcement operation that involves a cop in a plane to spot and clock speeders, and a cop on the ground to pull them over and write them a ticket.

Airspeed–The rate of an object (usually a plane) in relation to the air it is moving in.

Alcohol Abuse Class–Class you are usually required to attend following a drunk driving conviction.

Alcohol Impaired–When your balance, coordination and motor skills are compromised by the effects of alcohol.

Alleged–Charged with, but not found guilty of.

American Association of State Highway and Transportation Officials (AASHTO)–Group of officials who, between them, control most of what happens concerning our nations roadways.

Antagonist–Bad guy.

Appeal–Taking your case to a higher court after losing.

Appear–Show up in court.

Arbitrarily–Without good reason

Arraignment–Preliminary court proceeding where you enter motions or a plea, and pay your fine if you plead guilty.

Attorney General–The highest ranking law enforcement official in a state.

BAC Test–Test that determines the actual level of alcohol in your body. There are three of them. The blood test, the urine test and the breath test.

Bail–The face value of your ticket. Also the amount of money you must deposit with the court as good faith that you will return on your scheduled trial date.

Blood Alcohol Content (BAC)–The percentage of alcohol in your bloodstream.

Bra–Protective cover that wraps around the front of a vehicle to protect it from rocks, bugs and other flying debris.

Breathalyzer–The unit used to administer the breath BAC test.

Bureaucrats–Government officials.

Calibrate–To test for accuracy.

Call For Backup–What a cop will do if he thinks he might need assistance from other offers.

CB–Short for citizens band, a radio frequency that is available for anyone to communicate on. Mostly used by cops, truckers, and auto enthusiasts. Also refers to the radio unit itself.

Center Divider–The median that separates opposing sides of traffic on a roadway.

Certified Mail–Piece of mail that must be signed by the receiving party before it is released to them. Used when the sender must have proof that the other party received the piece of mail.

Change Of Venue–Moving your case to a different court.

Citation–"Politically correct" word for " ticket."

Cite–The act of an officer writing you a ticket.

Citing Officer– Cop who gave you the ticket.

City Planning Department–Local agency that handles zoning and building permits among other things.

Civil Lawsuit–Legal action filed by an injured party with the intent of obtaining compensation for damages.

Clock–Term used by law enforcement that refers to obtaining a speed reading on a vehicle.

Conviction–A case you lost.

Cop–Common nickname for a police officer.

County Seat–"Capitol" of a county.

Court Clerk–The person you usually wait in line to talk to when you first get to court. They tell you what to do and where to go.

Court Date–Day on which you are to appear in court.

Courtesy Notice–Notice sent out to ticket recipients by a court reminding them of an upcoming court date. It gives them the option of paying a specified bail amount in lieu of going to court.

Cross–Examination–When you get to ask a cop questions after he has finished his testimony.

Default–Victory as a result of your opponent not showing.

Defendant–Individual charged with a violation. Probably you.

Deflect–Bounce off in a different direction.

Diagram–Illustration.

Disclaimer–Release of liability.

Dismissal–When a ticket case is decided in your favor.

Dome Light–The light inside your vehicle directly above and to the right of your head.

Driver Training Class–Class you took, or should have taken, when you received your learners permit.

Driver's License–A card issued by a motor vehicle agency certifying that you may legally operate a motor vehicle.

Driving Record–A record kept by your motor vehicle agency of all tickets and accidents attributed to you that are reported to them.

Drone Radar–Unmanned radar transmitters whose sole purpose is to trigger radar detectors causing traffic to slow down.

Drunk–Same as alcohol impaired except worse.

DUI–Acronym for "driving under the influence."

DWI–Acronym for "driving while intoxicated."

Escape Clause–Special exception.

Extension–Continuance. Putting off your court date.

Failure To Appear– Violation you are charged with when you do not show up for your court date. Also referred to as an FTA.

FCC License–What every law enforcement agency must have in order to use radar.

Federal Communications Commission (FCC)–Government agency that has jurisdiction over every form of communication and transmission you could ever dream of. In the scope of this book the FCC has control over every aspect of radar.

Federal Highway Administration (FHA)–Government agency responsible for maintaining our highways and freeways.

Felony–The most serious classification of a violation.

Final Statement–What you give the judge right before he makes his decision. It is usually a summation of your arguments.

Fine–The amount that the judge orders you to pay on a ticket when you are found guilty.

Fix It Ticket–Slang for "repair ticket."

Flow Of Traffic–Speed at which most of the cars around you are traveling.

Frequency–Refers to band at which a radio signal is broadcast at.

Frolicking–Having a good time.

Ground Speed–The rate of an object (usually a vehicle) in relation to the ground it is traveling on.

Guilty Plea–When you admit to the offense you are charged with.

High Gloss Coat–Layer of transparent substance that is highly reflective.

Ignition Interlock–Device connected to a vehicle's ignition that measures blood alcohol levels. If the driver upon attempting to start the vehicle registers a higher than legal BAC level, the car will not start.

Impersonating–Appearing to be someone who you are not.

Impounded–Refers to your vehicle being taken away from you and stored at your expense. Usually a punishment associated with a DUI offense.

Intermittent Radar–Refers to

a cop who turns his radar unit on only when clocking someone instead of leaving it on all the time. This enables him to cut down on early warnings to drivers with radar detectors.

Invasion Of Privacy–When someone sticks their nose in your business.

Issuing Officer–The cop who wrote the ticket.

Jargon–Wording that is difficult to understand.

Judge–The person at the front of the courtroom who makes the final decision on your case.

Jurisdiction–The area that a court or law enforcement agency has power over.

Jury–A group of selected citizens who between them decide whether you are guilty or not after hearing your case.

Kindling–What photo radar tickets are good for.

Lack Of Prosecution–Condition that occurs when you show up for court and the officer doesn't.

Learners Permit–Card issued by a motor vehicle agency allowing you to operate a motor vehicle under specific condi-

tions while learning how to drive.

Legal BAC Level–Threshold at which you are considered legally drunk.

Legible–Readable.

Lidar–Also referred to as laser. New law enforcement weapon for measuring speed. Differs from radar in that it uses light waves (lasers) instead of radio waves.

Lidar Detectors–Devices designed to warn a motorist of lidar being used nearby.

Limit Line–Line marking the entrance to an intersection. Usually the furthest crosswalk line.

Limit Line Sensor–Beam directed across a limit line. When broken, it triggers a camera. A ticket is then mailed to the offending vehicle's registered owner via the license plate number.

Infraction–The least serious classification of a violation. Most tickets are infractions.

Loophole–Same as escape clause.

Misdemeanor–Classification of violation that is more serious than an infraction but less serious than a felony.

Mothers Against Drunk Drivers (MADD)–Organization that for several years has been lobbying against drunk driving and for tougher laws and enforcement pertaining to DUIs.

Motions–Actions you request of a court.

Motorist–Operator of a motor vehicle.

Moving Violation– Violation that has something to do with the actual way in which you were operating a motor vehicle.

Municipal Court–Court where minor violations such as infractions and misdemeanors are dealt with.

Municipality–Refers to an area of jurisdiction, usually local.

National Highway Traffic Safety Administration–Government agency whose role is to promote safety on our highways in any way possible.

National Maximum Speed Limit Law–Law stating that it is illegal to exceed a speed of 55 m.p.h. (65 m.p.h. on some freeways and highways) in a motor vehicle.

Negate–Same as nullify.

No Contest Plea–Same as not guilty plea except your plea cannot be used as evidence against you in the event that an injured party sues you as a result of an accident.

Non–Moving Violation–Violation that is related to the actual state of a vehicle or its location.

Not Guilty Plea–When you state that you did not commit the offense you are charged with.

Notice To Appear–Another designation for " ticket" or " citation." Does not apply to any ticket that you do not sign.

Nullify–To void or render powerless.

Obscure–Difficult to see or find.

Officer–(Pronounced "oshifer" when drunk) A euphemism for " cop."

On–Ramp–Entrance to a freeway.

Opt–Choose.

Ordinance–Another word for "law" or "code." Usually indicates a local law.

Overpass–Bridge over a freeway.

Pacing–When a officer travels at the same rate as you to determine your speed.

Parking Ticket–Ticket issued when a vehicle is left unattended in violation of a parking ordinance.

Patrol Car–Law enforcement vehicle.

Patrol Planes–Aircraft used by law enforcement to assist ground units in identifying speeders.

Photo Radar–Speed enforcement device that utilizes a radar gun, a computer and a camera to catch speeders on film. Tickets are mailed to the photographed vehicle's registered owner via the license plate number.

Plea Bargaining– Pleading guilty to a lesser charge in exchange for having the more serious charge dropped.

Plead–How you respond to charges when you go to court. Your choices are: guilty, not guilty and no contest.

Posted Speed Limit–Maximum legal speed on a roadway as designated by signs along the side of the road.

Pre trial Motions–Actions you request of a court at arraignment or before trial.

Prima Facie Speed Limits–Posted speed limits that may be legally exceeded if the road and other influencing conditions safely allow for it.

Probable Cause–Reason to believe. Good indication of. What an officer must have in order to stop you, search your vehicle or subject you to a BAC test.

Problem Drinker–Alcoholic. One who has trouble controlling their alcohol consumption.

Proceedings–Events that happen in a courtroom.

Promise To Appear–What you do when you sign the bottom of a citation.

Public Records Law–Law that allows you to request copies of documents such as traffic and engineering surveys and FCC licenses. Also allows you to obtain things like radar detectors and tuning forks.

Punitive Damages–Judgments awarded above and beyond any actual losses or damages incurred. They usually encompass things like pain and suffering.

Pupil–The center of your eye which adjusts for intensity of light by opening and closing accordingly.

Quota–The amount of tickets a cop is expected to write during a given time period.

Radar Cheating–When a cop falsifies his radar reading to secure speeding tickets. Usually occurs when a cop is behind in the ticket race.

Radar Detector–Device that is designed to warn a motorist when radar is being used nearby.

Radar Guns–Devices used by law enforcement to measure vehicle speed utilizing radio waves.

Radar Training Certificate–What an officer receives when he satisfactorily completes a course on how to use and operate a radar unit.

Red Tape–A seemingly useless mountain of forms to fill out, calls to make and lines to wait in. Generally encountered when dealing with any government agency.

Reflect–Bounce straight back.

Registered Owner–Person to whom the title of a vehicle belongs.

Registration–Document that you receive from your motor vehicle agency listing you as the owner of your vehicle. It also lists the vehicle's identification number, license plate number and other pertinent information.

Relevant–Related.

Repair Ticket–Citation issued when some part of your vehicle is not functioning correctly, or up to standard.

Residential District–Generally an area with a high concentration of homes.

Restricted License–Permit to drive a motor vehicle under certain conditions only. Usually to and from school and or work.

Road Hazards– Cops with radar guns.

Roadblock–Operation where law enforcement blocks a roadway and stops everyone on that road. The purpose is to catch drunk drivers.

Roadside Sobriety Test–A series of coordination exercises which suspected drunk drivers are subjected to. Cops use them to determine to what extent the motorist is under the influence of alcohol.

Section–Refers to a specific law within the vehicle code.

Social Drinker–One who has a drink or two at dinner or social functions, but has control over his/her consumption.

Speed Limit–Fastest speed legally allowed on a given road, at a given time and under given conditions.

Speed Trap–Any method that a cop uses to secure speeding violations in an unethical manner. It usually involves the use of VASCAR or a ridiculously low posted speed limit.

Squad Car–Equivalent of a police car.

Stone Cold Sober–Not under the influence of alcohol in any way.

Subpoena–To request a court to order some body of evidence to appear or be brought to court. Can also refer to the order itself.

Summons–Order to show up in court.

Summons Server–Someone who physically gives you a summons, this is usually a Marshal.

Superior Court–Place where serious offenses such as felonies, as well as appeals from lower courts, are heard.

Suspended License–An invalid license. Operating a motor vehicle with one of these is unlawful.

Swoop–Refers to a common maneuver used by cops to nab speeders on a freeway. The cop enters a freeway from an on-–ramp sneaking up behind you obtains a quick pace and pulls you over.

Testimony–Information given by anyone during a trial.

Ticket–Piece of paper received when cited by a law enforcement officer for violating a code.

Traffic And Engineering Survey–Study usually performed by transportation engineers to determine how the flow of traffic on a given roadway is interacting with the road itself as well as the surrounding influencing factors. Also used to determine the 85th percentile speed and, in turn, the posted speed limit.

Traffic Control Device–Stoplight, stop sign, roundabout or anything else used to regulate the flow of traffic.

Traffic Court–Place where vehicle code offense cases are heard and decided.

Traffic School–Place you go to learn about driving after you get your license. Attending traffic school can omit tickets from your driving record in many municipalities.

Traffic Stop–When an officer pulls over a motorist on charges of violating the vehicle code.

Transportation Engineer–Technician who studies all facets of transportation. Specifically in this book, one dealing with roadways and traffic.

Trial–The process of presenting and having your case decided in a court of law.

Trial By Declaration– Trial where you write out your case and arguments, including all of your supporting evidence, and mail them to the judge. The judge makes a decision and then mails it back.

Trooper–Another name for a cop. It is more commonly used when describing a highway patrolman.

Tuning Fork–Device used to test the accuracy of a radar unit.

U–Turn–180–degree turn.

U.S. Department Of Transportation–Government agency that has jurisdiction over anything and everything that is related to transportation.

Under The Influence–Same as alcohol impaired except it can refer to substances other than alcohol.

Unmarked Cars–Law enforcement vehicles that do not have any of the familiar identifying characteristics such as lights on the roof, agency insignia on the side, black and white paint job, etc. They will look like civilian vehicles except that they may have a driver side spotlight retracted inside the vehicle.

VASCAR–Device composed of a computer and a clock that calculate speeds by measuring time and distance.

Vehicle Code–Book full of laws governing the use of motor vehicles. Can also refer to a single vehicle law.

Violation–Act of disobeying a law or code.

Visual Estimation–Phrase an officer uses to get away with sounding intelligent when all he really did was guess how fast you were going.

Warrant–Order usually issued by a judge to have you arrested and brought to court. Also: Permission to search given to law enforcement by a judge. Commonly known as a search warrant.

Witness–Someone who was present when your alleged violation occurred. Usually a passenger.

Zero–Tolerance Law–Law that prohibits driving with any alcohol in your blood at all.

Index

ORDER FORM

Phone Orders: Call 1-800-322-6946
Fax Orders: Call 1-805-963-1644

Mail Orders: AceCo Publishers
924 Chapala St.
Suite D
Santa Barbara, CA 93101

Please send me _____ copies of "Beat The Cops"

Company Name: _____

Name: _____

Address: _____

City: _____

State: _____   Zip: _____

Price: $14.95 + $2.00 Postage and Handling
Priority Mail: Please add $3
Overnight: Please add $15

Payment: ☐ Check   ☐ Money Order   ☐ Visa   ☐ MC

Card #:   -   -   -   exp.

Signature: _____

☐   Please notify me when "Beat The Cops" is available on audio cassette.
☐   Please notify me when "Beat The Cops" is available in Spanish.

CALL *TOLL FREE* AND ORDER NOW!